THE
SACRED RITE
OF
MAGICAL LOVE

THE
SACRED RITE
OF
MAGICAL LOVE

A CEREMONY OF
WORD AND FLESH

MARIA DE NAGLOWSKA

Translated from the French with an
Introduction and Notes
by Donald Traxler

Inner Traditions
Rochester, Vermont • Toronto, Canada

Inner Traditions
One Park Street
Rochester, Vermont 05767
www.InnerTraditions.com

SUSTAINABLE FORESTRY INITIATIVE Certified Sourcing

www.sfiprogram.org

SFI-00854

Text stock is SFI certified

Translation, introduction, and commentary © 2012 by Donald C. Traxler

Originally published in French in 1932 as a supplement of *La Flèche: Organe d'Action Magique* under the title *Le Rite sacré de l'amour magique*

All rights reserved. No part of this book may be reproduced or utilized in any form or by any means, electronic or mechanical, including photocopying, recording, or by any information storage and retrieval system, without permission in writing from the publisher.

Library of Congress Cataloging-in-Publication Data

Naglowska, Maria de, 1883–1936.

[Rite sacré de l'amour magique. English]

The sacred rite of magical love : a ceremony of word and flesh / Maria de Naglowska ; translated from the French with an introduction and notes by Donald Traxler.

p. cm.

Includes bibliographical references (p.   ) and index.

ISBN 978-1-59477-417-1 (pbk.) — ISBN 978-1-59477-706-6 (e-book)

I. Traxler, Donald. II. Title.

PQ2627.A38R58 2012

843'.912—dc23

2011035918

Printed and bound in the United States by Lake Book Manufacturing

The text stock is SFI certified. The Sustainable Forestry Initiative® program promotes sustainable forest management.

10 9 8 7 6 5 4 3 2 1

Text design and layout by Priscilla Baker

This book was typeset in Garamond Premier Pro with Democratica used as a display typeface

This [the magical union of man and woman] is
a great mystery for the profane, and the
most beautiful light for the initiate.

MARIA DE NAGLOWSKA

CONTENTS

Introduction: A Life of Magic and Mystery
by Donald Traxler ix

Preface: A Key that Opens Doors 1

1 In the Mist of Thought 7

2 The Birth to Love 15

3 The Baptism 28

4 The Test 39

5 Joy on the Plain 49

6 The Crossing 72

7 On the Other Shore 82

8 About the New Religion: The Doctrine of the
Third Term of the Trinity 93

Appendix A. The Two Editions of the Story   99

Appendix B. The Aum Clock   104

Appendix C. Naglowska's Sources   108

Notes   113

Bibliography   115

Index   118

INTRODUCTION

A LIFE OF MAGIC AND MYSTERY

Donald Traxler

T*he Sacred Rite of Magical Love* is the third in our series of works by Maria de Naglowska. It is an initiatic novelette, probably partly autobiographical. It was first serialized in the first eight issues of Naglowska's street newspaper, *La Flèche, organe d'action magique,* from October 15, 1930, to December 15, 1931. Naglowska published the serialization under the pseudonym Xenia Norval.* She republished it as a supplement to her newspaper in the spring of 1932, this time using her real name. She sold this

---

*[Naglowska's choice of the name Xenia is, no doubt, a reference to Blessed Xenia of Saint Petersburg, a saint of the Russian Orthodox Church. The parallels between Blessed Xenia's life and Maria de Naglowska's life are astonishing. Both women were married to musicians, and both were thrown into a life of hardship by the loss of their husbands (to Zionism, in Naglowska's case) at about age twenty-seven. In their lives of poverty, their spirituality was their greatest comfort. —*Trans.*]

supplement with subscriptions to her newspaper, at her lectures, through the mail, and probably also on the streets of Montparnasse. It is both more personal and more mysterious than her other works.

Who was this woman who tirelessly wrote, published, and spoke to share her spiritual vision with the world?

Maria de Naglowska was born in St. Petersburg in 1883, the daughter of a prominent Czarist family.* She went to the best schools and got the best education that a young woman of the time could get. She fell in love with a young Jewish musician, Moise Hopenko, and married him against the wishes of her family. The ensuing rift with Maria's family caused the young couple to leave Russia, going to Germany and then to Switzerland. After Maria had given birth to three children, her young husband, a Zionist, decided to leave his family and go to Palestine. This made things very difficult for Naglowska, who was forced to take various writing, translating, and journalism jobs to make ends meet. While she was living in Geneva she translated a book of philosophy from French to Russian,†

---

*[I have drawn most of the details about Naglowska's life from the short biography titled *La Sophiale,* written by her favorite student, Marc Pluquet. It is, by far, the most reliable source. —*Trans.*]

†[*Une révolution dans la philosophie,* by Frank Grandjean. The subject is the philosophy of Henri Bergson, who influenced Naglowska greatly. In the preface to the second edition there is a note stating that the first edition had been translated into Russian by "Mme Marie Naglowska" and that it was for sale in the "principal cities of Russia."[1] —*Trans.*]

she wrote a French grammar for Russian immigrants to Switzerland,* and she reported on the Geneva peace talks that ended World War I.† Unfortunately, Naglowska's libertarian ideas tended to get her into trouble with governments wherever she went. She spent the first part of the 1920s in Rome, where from 1921 to 1926 she worked on the review *L'Italia*. In 1927 she moved to Alexandria, Egypt, where she wrote for one publication‡ and directed another.§

While in Rome, Maria de Naglowska met Julius Evola, a pagan traditionalist. Evola was also an occultist, being a member of the Group of Ur and counting among his associates some of the followers of Giuliano Kremmerz. It is said that Naglowska and Evola were lovers. It is known, at least, that they were associates for a long time. She translated one of his poems ("La parole obscure du paysage intérieur; poème à 4 voix") into French (the only form in which it has survived), and he later translated some of her work into Italian.

While occultists give a great deal of weight to Naglowska's relationship with Evola, it is clear that there must have been

---

*[*Nouvelle méthode de la langue française,* by "Marie de Naglowska." —*Trans.*]

†[*La paix et son principale obstacle,* by "Mariya Naglovskaya." —*Trans.*]

‡[*La Réforme,* 1927–28. —*Trans.*]

§[*Alexandrie Nouvelle,* 1928–29. —*Trans.*]

other influences.* Some believe that she was influenced by the Russian sect of the Khlysti, and some believe that she knew Rasputin (whose biography she translated). Maria, though, gave the credit for some of her unusual ideas to an old Catholic monk whom she met in Rome. Although Maria said that he was quite well known there, he has never been identified.

Maria said that the old monk gave her a piece of cardboard on which was drawn a triangle to represent the Trinity. The first two apexes of the triangle were clearly labeled to indicate the Father and the Son. The third, left more indistinct, was intended to represent the Holy Spirit. To Maria, the Holy Spirit was feminine. We don't know how much was the monk's teaching and how much was hers, but Maria taught that the Father represented Judaism and reason, while the Son represented Christianity, the heart, and an era whose end was approaching. To Maria, the feminine Spirit represented a new era, sex, and the reconciliation of the light and dark forces in nature.

It is mostly this idea of the reconciliation of the light and dark forces that has gotten Maria into trouble and caused her to be thought of as a Satanist. Maria herself is partly

*[Some of these other influences are examined in appendix C. —*Trans.*]

responsible for this, having referred to herself as a "satanic woman" and used the name also in other ways in her writings. Evola, in his book *The Metaphysics of Sex,* mentioned her "deliberate intention to scandalize the reader." Here is what Naglowska herself had to say about it.

> We forbid our disciples to imagine Satan (= the spirit of evil or the spirit of destruction) as living outside of us, for such imagining is proper to idolaters; but we recognize that this name is true.

In 1929 Naglowska moved to Paris, where she got the unwelcome news that she would not be given a work permit. Deprived of the ability to be employed in a regular job, she would have to depend on her own very considerable survival skills. She first worked as cotranslator of a biography of Rasputin, which was published in 1930.[2] She then began work on the book for which she is best known today, her "translation" of *Magia Sexualis* by Paschal Beverly Randolph. This work by the American hermetist and sex theorist is known only in Naglowska's "translation," which was published in 1931.[3] I have put the word "translation" in quotation marks because it is really a compilation. Only about two-thirds of the work can be identified as being from Randolph. The rest is from sources only beginning to be identified, or from Naglowska herself, and the organization of the material is clearly her contribution as well.

While Naglowska was working on *Magia Sexualis,* she began giving lectures or "conferences" on an original teaching of her own. She called it the Doctrine of the Third Term of the Trinity. Her "conferences" were at first often held in cafés. The proprietors of these venues were pleased with the influx of patrons and often gave Maria free food and coffee. In a short time her following grew to the point where she could afford to rent a large, bare room, which held thirty to forty people, for her private meetings. It was thus that Maria survived.

Maria's income was supplemented by her publishing endeavors. In late 1930 she began publishing a little newspaper, to which she and other occultists contributed, called *La Flèche, Organe d'Action Magique.* It was the public voice of her magical group, *La Confrérie de la Flèche d'Or.*

In late 1932 Naglowska published *La Lumière du sexe,*[4] published in English in the current series as *The Light of Sex.*[5] In 1934 she published *Le Mystère de la pendaison,*[6] published in this English series as *Advanced Sex Magic: The Hanging Mystery Initiation.*[7] These two books were required reading for even First Degree initiation into Naglowska's magical group and contained all of the doctrine of her new religion, the Third Term of the Trinity, and much of its ritual. They are thus of paramount importance for understanding Maria de Naglowska and her teaching. They are also, unfortunately, quite rare, as is the present work, having been originally published in small editions of about five hundred copies. To my knowledge the translations in the present series are the first that have been made of any of Naglowska's original works into English.

Naglowska is said to have been very psychic. She predicted the catastrophe of the Second World War, and in 1935 she foresaw her own death. Knowing that she was going to die, she refused to reprint *The Light of Sex* and *The Hanging Mystery,* which had both sold out. She told her followers that nothing would be able to be done to spread her teachings for two or three generations. She went to live with her daughter, Marie Grob, in Zurich, and it was there that she died, at the age of 52, on April 17, 1936.

Maria was influential among the Surrealists, and they seem to have influenced her own writing. Naglowska's French was impeccable and her style clean and powerful, but she used words in a symbolic, highly idiosyncratic way. Shortly before she left Paris, she told her disciples that her teachings "would need to be translated into clear and accessible language for awakened women and men who would not necessarily be symbolists." Taking this as my directive, I have added extensive explanatory footnotes to the texts of all these books.

Due to the small editions and her refusal to reprint them, plus her early death and the unfortunate arrival of World War II, Maria's influence seems hardly to have extended beyond Montparnasse. This is now changing. With the perspective granted by time we can see that Naglowska was an important mystic of the twentieth century. It is hoped that the present book and the two that preceded it will help us to better understand this mysterious woman and her vision, which is one of upliftment for humanity.

DONALD TRAXLER began working as a professional translator (Benemann Translation Service, Berlitz Translation Service) in 1963. Later, he did translations for several institutions in the financial sector. On his own time he translated poetry and did his first metaphysical translations in the early 1980s. He later combined these interests, embarking on an ambitious, multiyear project to translate the works of Lalla (also known as Lalleshvari, or Lal Ded), a beloved fourteenth-century poet of Kashmir Shaivism. That project is still not complete, but many of the translations have become favorites of contemporary leaders of the sect. He is currently focusing on Western mysticism: *The Sacred*

Rite of Magical Love is the third of a five-book series by Maria de Naglowska for Inner Traditions. He is contemplating a major project on another European mystic and an eventual return to and completion of the Lalla project. Except for Lalla, he translates from Spanish, French, and Italian. All of his projects are labors of love.

THE SACRED RITE

Of

MAGICAL LOVE

L'HORLOGE AVM

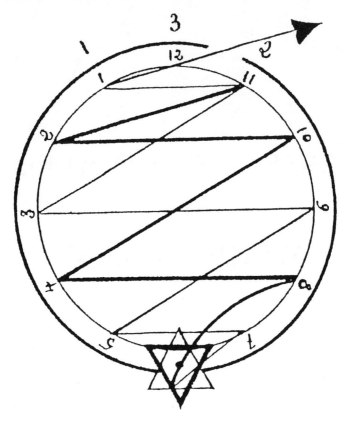

2 à 6 = CHUTE   = A

■ = UNION MAGIQUE = V

6 à 1 = ÉLÉVATION   = M

The AUM Clock.
Fall, Magical Union, and Elevation

preface

A KEY THAT
OPENS DOORS

The symbol on the facing page has tremendous power. It is a talisman for every person who delves into its mystery with respect.

The symbol is neither an image reproducing this or that particular thing or idea, nor an inscription in the limited sense.

The symbol is a key that opens doors, but it is still necessary to have the capacity to see the treasures hidden behind those doors.

The symbol that we are here offering to the public bears the name "AUM CLOCK."

It is the key that permits one to understand that the same Law presides over the birth of a child, over the rebirth of an individual dead to material life and remade for spiritual life, and over the triple change of the visible world, which repeats unceasingly, according to an eternal rhythm: the evening, the night, and the new morning.

This rhythm corresponds to the successive and eternal phases of Divinity, the Life of which manifests sometimes under the aspect of the Father, sometimes under that of the Son, and sometimes under the aspect of the Mother. First there is the Fall, immediately followed by the Struggle against the Fall, and lastly the Victory of the Divine Renewal through Mother Nature.

But the Renewal, which lasts only a short time, determines a new Fall, followed by a new Struggle, and so on eternally. The high wisdom of this disinterested Will always escapes the vulgar spirit, which only acts for its own interest, but the purified individual sees the beauty of it.

The AUM CLOCK, which comes to us from India and Egypt, and whose virtue we ourselves have experienced, is constructed as follows:

First of all there is a clock dial, like all those in the world but always with this difference, that the movement of the hours is assumed to be from right to left, and not from left to right as is the case for sundials.*

At eleven o'clock the Fall begins. It is indicated on our

---

*[It should be noted that this right-to-left numbering corresponds to that of astrological charts drawn for the Northern Hemisphere. The AUM clock is discussed further in appendix B. —*Trans.*]

design by the thick, black line that, starting from the number 11, passes successively to 2, to 10, to 4, and to 8 to finally penetrate into the number 6, represented here by the Seal of Solomon, that is to say by the two interlaced triangles, which symbolize the Fall of Divinity into Matter (or Nature) and the Will toward Spiritual Renewal of the latter through mankind.

This same symbol, as also the complete AUM design, represents respiration as well, which is composed of inhaling, exhaling, and rest.

The line that is broken at 2, 10, 4, and 8 is the feminine line, because the Fall operates through the woman and in the woman for the man, and in Nature, for God.

Every student of Wisdom should meditate at length on this essential Truth.

But why is the line of the Fall broken, and why does the feminine path pass through the 2, the 10, the 4, and the 8? In other words, what do these numbers mean?

The knowledge that we possess answers thus:

Eleven symbolizes the Entry (of the man into the woman, and of God into Nature), 2 represents the marriage of the two opposite elements and, consequently, the departure point for a new orientation. It is the formation of an angle.

The number 10, being the result of the multiplication of 2 by 5, and these two signifying respectively the feminine and the masculine, we have, in our design, at hour 10, a sort of defeat of Man, precipitated from this instant, with Woman, into the depths of Hell (Matter).

At hour 4, the two opposite elements are equal. There is then the crucifixion of the Spirit on the Sacred Wood of Nature; it is the sorrow of the man who abdicates and it is the suffering of the fertilized woman. Then a new angle orients the black road toward the 8.

This number signifies the first day of the new period, in which the woman dominates the man, while Matter imprisons the Spirit in the depths of its entrails. We are, at hour 8, at the edge of the pit, in which one dies or is reborn.

The number 6, which is the limit of the Fall, determines Rebirth.

This is a great mystery for the profane and the most beautiful light for the initiate.

The individual belongs to sin, but he who rises up again, from that moment, is reborn to eternal life.

This passage is dangerous for many men, but the Son of God triumphs and is reborn. It is the mystery of the Victory of the Christ.

From 7 to 5, and from 5 to 9, then from 9 to 3, and from 3 to 11, the Victorious One rises again in spirituality, according to the lighter line of our design. At each angle (and these are the masculine angles), the spiritual virtues of the man grow, and he arrives before the Door (number 11), strengthened by new powers.

Meanwhile, before this door, the supreme test awaits him. Here the man sees the woman again, his wife. He is invited to again plunge himself into her, but he remains dry, that is to say he prevents the sexual energy from crystallizing in order to offer it totally to the Spirit. This test is very dangerous, for a fall at this instant brings with it loss of reason.

But the Victorious One is immediately projected into one, which determines or signifies his liberation from the prison of matter. He is the sacred King and acquires the power to govern men . . .

The Sacred Rite of Magical Love is the story of the natural formation of such a King.

We offer this book for the meditation of the readers, because too many different methods today tend to facilitate the Royal Magical Experience by artificial means that flatter pride but offend God and lead only to half-results, called "scientific."

The perfect result lights the three stars of Wisdom, represented in our design by the numbers 1, 3, and 2, arranged respectively above the 1, the 12, and the 11 of the dial. In their turn, these Stars form the Divine Triangle, composed of the Father, the Son, and the Mother; but in our story the 3 (the Star of the Mother) and the 2 (the Star of the Son) are the only ones lighted, because our heroes (Misha and Xenia) haven't yet accomplished the rite, still more important, of the Second Marriage, which is reserved for the formation of the Messiah.

(1 = 5)

This last Star, which is called the brilliant Morning Star, does not belong to our epoch, because our suffering has not yet ended: humanity is just beginning its elevation toward Spirit, and the era of the Third Term must pass before the coming to our earth of the Messiah-King.

MARIA DE NAGLOWSKA

IN THE MIST Of
THOUGHT

We are born to be happy. Our natural destiny is balance, harmony, for if we were what we should be, the whole universe would be reflected in each of us as a splendid chant: joyous, triumphant. And the earth would speak to us in its language full of wisdom, which would guide us through life. And the sky would be for us a continual and tender caress, and its rain would be a blessing, and its light an instruction. And from afar, from the four points of the horizon, the winds would bring us the necessary breath that reanimates, that fortifies, that vivifies. And the great sea, blue or green or mauve, would have no more mystery for us, and its furious waves would not frighten us—if we were what we are destined to be—normal men and women.

But there is something in the world that keeps us from being normal. There is a force in the world that stubbornly hinders life, and the song of the universe, because of that, contains dissonances that sow sorrow, falsity, and cruelty.

There is a vast wickedness spread through the world. It prevents men from being men and women from being women. And the children themselves cannot be children, naive, fresh, joyous, because of this wickedness that howls through beings as an inconsolable desperation. The most diverse names have been given to this malicious force, for people have always sought to paralyze it.

They called it Satan, they made the devil out of it, they said that it was the spirit-of-evil, or the spirit-of-destruction, and I don't know what else! None of these names were in any way real, and that is why the Enemy was not subdued.

For here is what is certain although strange: it would suffice to discover the true name (the essential correspondence) of the wickedness to localize it and make it disappear. It is a mystery, because it is difficult to explain in vulgar terms the life and the essence of names, but it is true that if one knew how to pronounce, that is to say to fulfill, the rite symbolizing the Supreme Hindrance, all its malefic force would be paralyzed. Better still: it would no longer exist.

Ah! If you could understand that, or rather, decipher it after the reading of this book, which is written with this in mind! The evil force that hinders the triumphal march of the future is none other than the Past, incapable of dying because nothing dies. It awaits its regeneration, the baptism that will change its name. New lips are necessary for that, because "an old name pronounced by a new mouth is a new name, a rebirth . . ."

What precautions are needed, alas, in these troublesome times, to say the simplest things! We live in an epoch in which many contrary currents meet with equal violence. It is like those places on the sea where the ships dance even in good weather. We no longer understand each other, the vocabulary differs from mouth to mouth, one says "spirit" and the other understands "humbug."

At the same time, in this life we are only so many leaves offered to the sun and the fresh air. Deep roots, which connect all of us to the same earth, bring us the sap that the Sun itself has blessed, but Man makes poor use of it, because he no longer knows anything . . .

And one will understand this: I have loved the Malefic One, I love him still, that is why I know his Name, his Essence, his nocturnal action . . .

On the wild peaks of the silent Caucasus, in the rocky valleys of its ranges whence have come the races and peoples whose mission was and still is to combat evil, I have seen the huge shadow of the Master of the Past cross its arms in a tortured attitude.

Snakes were biting his flattened belly and a sticky muck rose up to his thighs.

He fixed his gaze on the roses blooming in my garden and icy tears burned his eyes.

"Oh!" he cried, in a sepulchral voice, "Oh! Xenophonta! The empire was mine! The waters came, they drowned my lands and my gardens with the golden grapes. My flocks are dead in the debacle and my servants are scattered. I no longer have anything to offer you; I no longer have any gold to buy you with."

And those last words resounded in the dry night of the mountains as a bitter reproach, as an immense hatred.

I was stricken by love because of this terrible cry, I adored this unfathomable powerlessness.

"Who are you? O you who weep for your fortune!" I said, terrified.

"I am he whose name cannot be uttered, for the language that contained it is forgotten . . . Xenophonta, I cannot buy you, and so you will not be my wife."

The specter disappeared in a wild howling of the wind, which came up then like a prolonged rage of all nature. The roses of my garden trembled with it until morning.

At the dawn, when the storm had quieted itself in the steel blue of the first hours, I went out onto the terrace to again find him to whom my heart would henceforth belong. The mountains were the same, their lofty lines as severe and rigid as before, the snow still slept, scarcely blued by the reverberations of the sky, but in the cold breath of the forests and in the crystalline sounds of the torrents the Caucasus, *my* Caucasus, was not the same. Ah! Yes! The Master of the Past was there. "The lands, my lands are drowned." This cry was everywhere, and nothing could efface it.

A violent desire was born then in my body, and I would have cut open my insides if my blood spilled on the snow could have had the virtue of melting the ice and giving new birth to the pastures of the one who wept. But my blood was only a drop to this ocean of ice, and what could that drop do against so much unhappiness!

The Sun suddenly appeared. Still red from too long a sleep, its glare did not blind the eyes. Its face smiled between two peaks, and it seemed that the rocks palpitated with joy.

"Oh! Sun!" I said, persuaded of the human consciousness of the star, "won't you make this ice melt to bring back the riches that have disappeared?"

And, distinctly, I heard this answer: "You were his slave, but I have liberated you. It is to put the handcuffs back on you that he wants his goods. But he shall not have them. I want you free, woman, you and your children."

"Who is he?" I asked, and my hands were cold.

"His name is forgotten, and the language that, alone, contained it, will not be found again, for I have changed the throat of mortals, so that no syllable of that accursed word can ever again penetrate into a human brain and there disturb the course of things . . . Xenophonta, woe to you if you attach yourself to that deceased one."

The strident cry of an enormous bird of prey then interrupted the word of the Sun, and I heard a strange fall in the valley where an intense light now shone. The Sun had now gone from red to almost white, and my eyes could no longer support its glare.

The bird of prey glided in wide spirals above my parents' house. The strange thing is that it did not frighten me. I felt a protection within me, a force whose source I didn't know. And, as it turned out, after a few silent turns the bird changed its mind and flew away.

There was then a radiant smile in nature, and the sky and the snow and the roses participated in it.

The dew was cool on the terrace, and I felt a shiver along my legs. Involuntarily, I bent my knees, and my hands came together of their own accord for prayer. But my lips did not pronounce the customary words. What they said was approximately this:

Lord! Power! Life!

In this morning hour

Hear me!

My roses pray with me

And my blood vivifies my prayer.

Wipe away the icy tears

And also smother the fire.

Command that the wounds be closed up

And order that joy be for all.

Lord, forgive, for all my body forgives.

Pardon, O eternal Power,

Him who suffers and weeps incessantly.

Do not curse that which trembles in fear,

Draw into your immense joy

The shadow of the Past, the shadow of the
    Firstborn.

Change into good that which is evil

And change into virtue that which is
    fault.

Everywhere spread your unfathomable
    wisdom,

And forgive, O Power, that which I
    forgive.

For you are life and order and the song
    of joy.

For you are the river and your waters
  take all away.
Be merciful, O harmonious Trinity!
Forgive, forgive, forgive!

I was stretched out on the flagstones of the terrace when the last word of this prayer had closed my mouth. A long kiss still burned there.

THE BIRTH TO LOVE

The life of Man is not made up only of concrete facts and events that are accessible to ordinary observation. Often, the real experience is elsewhere, beyond the physical plane, but we forbid ourselves to admit that reality. Certainly, we thus impoverish ourselves enormously, and we deprive ourselves of the essential: of the capacity to communicate with the great forces spread out in nature. We limit our knowledge to that which is controlled by cerebral science, thus slowing down the rhythm of our life. We get old because of that, because we thus foul the channel that connects us to the root and to the only means by which we are permitted to participate in the eternal youth of the universe. We are like the leaf that becomes detached from the tree of life: "It shrivels and yellows and the wind carries it away at will."*

---

*[This appears to be a quotation, but I have not been able to identify it. —*Trans.*]

Adam detached the fruit of the Tree, he knew then what was right and left, high and low, long and short, but by this same act he generated the principle of immobility, Death, which from that time spread out over the earth. And so that he should no longer hear the voice of the cavern of the woman, he put a seal upon it: the first article of clothing. He said to Eve: "Thou shalt hide thyself from me, for thou art temptation."*

The woman remained silent and forgot the truth, but, in the generations that followed, faith in her victory remained intact . . . Lying prostrate on the flagstones of the terrace of my ancestors, before the majestic Kasbek, I felt this faith reignite itself in me as a new light; the ardent kiss of the Shadow had confirmed it for me.

I detached myself with some difficulty from the stones, already hot because the sun had followed its ascendant curve with the usual rapidity, and asked myself whether I should rejoin my family or instead go down into the garden to calm my feelings. But such was my disturbance that choosing between these alternatives was difficult for me.

The terrace had no direct communication with the living quarters inside. A rustic stairway, made of crude blocks, led from its north point to the east point of the large bal-

---

*[Source, if any, not identified. —*Trans.*]

cony of the ground floor, and from there, also to the north, a small ladder of iron allowed one to descend to the small court where the peacocks and geese of the lower yard paraded from morning until evening. A watchdog slept there too, in his free time.

I made an effort to glide like a thief in front of the doors and windows of the street level, in order to show myself to the animals before any encounter with humans . . . my roses drew me on, for I expected support from them.

I made this trip with extreme slowness, and I looked at the peacocks out of the corner of my eye for, certainly, I feared their reproach. But when I arrived at the lawn where my roses flourished, I began to run. Why? I had no idea.

In this wild country, where European civilization can have no foothold, because of the commercial uselessness of its rocks, a rapid course presents many dangers: there are deep and swift streams, enormous rocks that bar one's passage without warning, centuries-old tree trunks toppled by high winds and which no profane arm would be allowed to raise, for everyone respects these sacred cadavers: we know that they are altars, on which are accomplished mysteries that only the purest may witness.

How is it possible then that I was able to run this course without stopping a single time? Explain it as you will, but the truth is that I arrived in the forest shade in what seemed to me to be only a second. I stopped near a giant oak, as if someone had suddenly galvanized me, and I said in the most natural voice, "Here I am."

It was very hot, and the wind did not stir. Nature was perfectly still and as if paralyzed by the rays of the sun that shone everywhere through the leaves and branches. At the same time, a dull agitation filled everything: the atmosphere, the vegetation, the dry branches.

"Here I am," I said again, and an answer should have come, but it kept me waiting.

I understood that it was necessary to repeat it a third time.

"Look, I'm here, I'm listening," I said, as if that were necessary, and, indeed, a weak sigh reached my ears.

I still could not distinguish any word, and I stood more still.

"You have come, indeed, a faraway voice said, but you do not know me. You love, it is true, but not me, for you do not know who I am. There is something worse than that: the day that you shall know me, you will feel horror of me.

From the deepest part of my being, I gave assurance to the contrary.

The voice then had something like a flash of life, and it

almost seemed to me that I recognized a form. But the illusion immediately vanished.

"No, no, it is impossible for me to believe it now," I heard, and if I could only describe to you the sorrow that was in these words! "How can you love me, seeing that you do not know me?"

"Put me to the test," I said.

Again, I sensed a kind of joy in the invisible being, but this joy also vanished, like the first.

"Come here at one o'clock in the morning, when it will be cold, and only the serpents will dance about. Because you wish it, I shall test you, but know well that I do not believe in your strength."

Can you imagine my disappointment? Still, I adored the insult, as I had adored the powerlessness.

"Last night, while everything slept, you showed me your wound," I said timidly, "and your kiss burns me still. Would I have wanted you, if you hadn't shown yourself to me?"

Something sneered then very near me, and a green frog made a sudden pirouette. The branches of the old oak shuddered, and a small bird, disturbed, changed its place.

"Many things seem different by night," the Lord that I had implored began speaking again. "And I may permit myself certain promenades. But only that is true, which does not cease to be true."

This saying hushed me, and I felt myself to be infinitely small in front of this enormous something, which filled its spoken sentence with a limitless dignity. I was all wordless resignation.

"I shall wait for you, then, here, tonight, at one o'clock," were the last words that titillated my ears.

I leaned on the rough trunk of the oak, for what I felt at that moment was so full of charm that I wanted to let it penetrate into all my muscles, all my organs. Water penetrates thus into a sponge, which offers it no resistance.

A long quarter of an hour passed. I was still immobile, glued to the trunk of the oak, when a graceful animal, held up by delicate legs and covered with sleek, short hair, stopped in front of me. In its eyes, shaped like beautiful almonds, there shone a sweet mockery.

"What are you doing?" those eyes seemed to say. "At this hour, your place is not here."

Indeed, humans have their dwellings among the rocks, of which they build their houses. Man is the enemy of the wild and free beasts for which he represents prison.

The severe walls of the chateau of my ancestors called me back to my place.

When I was again near the balcony suspended over the little courtyard of the peacocks and geese, my family was already gathered together there for the meal; but such, in our house, was the liberty granted to the young girl who had finished her studies that no one was disturbed by seeing me wordlessly climb through the low window that was exactly in front of the iron ladder. I have told you that this was the north corner of the chateau. Don't forget it, for it has its importance: the north has a special magic.

The room into which I penetrated was a sort of ballroom. There were white and gold chairs lined up along the walls, and an enormous grand piano took up the whole southern corner.

No carpet, and no fabric over the windows.

From this hall, many doors opened upon the corridor that had to be crossed to arrive at the stairway that led to the floor where the different bedrooms were located. Mine was exactly above the ballroom, with six windows: three to the northeast, and three to the northwest. These windows had long, deep-blue curtains of embroidered cloth from the Ukraine.

The furnishings were very simple: a quite narrow bed in the inside corner, a robust chest of drawers, a few chairs, a small, Turkish divan, a writing table; in short, strictly what was necessary for someone who did not have much to do.

In the east corner, as is *de rigueur* among the Orthodox, the holy icons in their traditional triangular cupboard-table.

I went straight to the icons, and I knelt down in prayer.

What is prayer for a soul accustomed to the rite of the Eastern Church?

It is necessary that I spell it out, for those who shall read me will undoubtedly be Catholics or, at the least, people who have been taught according to the Catholic mentality. For them, for these presumed readers, prayer means obeying a law of the Church, of which only the leaders know what purpose it serves. Prayer, for the average Catholic, is the fulfilling of a duty in order to receive in exchange, protection or grace from Heaven.

It isn't, as for the Orthodox, an entry into direct communication with Divinity, of which we really drink the essence. It isn't this act of supplication without request that transports our soul and uplifts us, without it even being necessary to say or think the words.

Our prayer is not even called prayer. The word that we use, *molitva,* means "influence," and we experience it as designating a state of holiness where, worldly preoccupations being absent, we attract toward ourselves the power of Heaven.

Among us one prays as one sings, when one feels carried beyond the world, and that was definitely my case at the time of which I am speaking.

The icon that I focused on while praying was one of those

Byzantine images covered in old, darkened silver with which we are all familiar.

It represented St. Serge-of-the-Many-Miracles who, they say, was the first founder of monastic life in Russia. His face was barely visible, but the metal that made up his vestments shone mysteriously in the yellow glow of the votive lamp that burned night and day on the icon stand.

It is not very surprising, given the state in which I then found myself that in my eyes, the lightly marked face of Saint Serge took on unusual proportions.

His eyes became animated, and I felt a real look there. Certainly not that of the great Saint, but rather that of the Unknown to whom I had bound myself.

I would confess to you more than that. Little by little, my prayer, my *molitva,* became a veritable fusion of my inner being with the tortured Magician that I had adored now for a dozen hours. As the moments passed, this fusion was intensified, to such a point that I ended up feeling perfectly nonexistent, even corporeally.

The sweetness of this feeling is difficult to describe, for all words are too weak and too concrete in comparison with this marvelous state of absolute blessedness. Imagine a caress without any touch, a warmth that had nothing of the carnal, a multiple kiss that did not land anywhere. If you can imagine the very special enjoyment that comes from such a caress, you will have approximately the idea of what I felt at that moment, and you will agree with me that no ordinary mortal, that is to say made like everyone else, can plunge a woman into as great a state of delight.

All my being took pleasure in this voluptuous non-existence, and the force that inebriated me was without limits. It was the immensity of the Infinite that took me on while obliterating me, and I felt immense without being . . .

Oh! Why did the hall clock have to stupidly strike the hour, pulling me out of this bliss?

Three metallic strikes, indifferent, cold.

I jumped to my feet and looked all around me. The furniture had not moved: nothing in the bedroom had participated in my enchantment.

I stretched out on my bed and rang for my old servant.

She arrived very tranquilly, without knocking at the door, and said to me in her caressing voice, "Is it only now that you are getting an appetite?"

Indeed, I hadn't eaten since the night before.

"Give me some milk and some dark bread," I said.

She went away the way she had come, quite calmly, very slowly, and came back a half hour later with the food that I had asked her for.

"There are some guests in the drawing room," she said,

putting the plate down on a chair near the bed. "Some neighbors who will spend the night."

"Niania, tell my mother, if she is worried about me, that I won't be going down until tomorrow morning. Visiting bores me."

"As you wish, my little soul," the old woman answered. "But it is more likely that no one will ask anything, for you are on vacation and you have your freedom . . ."

"It's the south bedrooms that we are preparing for the visitors," she added.

"So much the better," I said, without quite knowing why . . .

Building houses according to an exact orientation with respect to the cardinal points of the horizon is an important thing that, nevertheless, the Europeans totally neglect, because they have lost the real sense of the cross that at the same time joins and divides the north, south, east, and west points.

The north is immobility, the absence of the eternally changing dynamism of life. It is the refuge of the intellect, for, alone, it allows to the latter the necessary repose for an abstract reflection without troubling it with new influences.

If there were only north, Man would know everything, for everything would be quite calm to permit him to see each thing in its smallest details.

It would be night, always, and Man would be its king.

The south is, on the contrary, the source of perpetual life. It is the point par excellence, which animates our most vital organs, those that the intellect is ashamed to see because they remind it unceasingly of its insufficiency: its incapacity to follow the vertiginous course of the Universe, its mobility, its capricious modifications.

If there were only south, there would be nothing on earth except wild beasts.

The intermediates, east and west, are the passages between the two extremes, and the east represents Man coming from Life and going to Stasis or Death, while the west is the point where Death turns to Life and prepares Rebirth. Still, west carries in its essence the elements of Death . . .

When a house is built in conformity with the science of the cardinal points of the horizon, one rests his head at night in the north and his feet in the south. In this way his intellect is really calmed during sleep, and Life, always fertile in the darkness, finds no obstacles to its penetration into the body according to the natural law: from the bottom up.

In addition, properly oriented, the slumbering body of the human being receives, through its right arm and its organs on the right side, the elements of the reconstructive push of the universal forces, while on its left—from its left arm and from its heart above all—the overflow escapes that is destined to die, that is to say to decompose to return to the Root, in the center of the Earth where the regenerating fire crackles . . .

All in good time you shall see the reason for these lines.

THE BAPTISM

When I had drunk the milk and eaten the black bread, and when the servant had left, after having told me again that the visitors, for whom we were preparing the south apartment, were the Wassilkowskys, father, mother, and son, and that there would be a ball in the evening, I felt the need to sleep.

So I pulled the six pairs of draperies on the six windows, the latter remaining wide open, and I took off the clothing that was constricting my body.

From the large chest of drawers I pulled a long dressing gown of unbleached cloth, strewn with embroidered arabesques—the squares, triangles, stars that make up what are called Russian designs but which are in reality the chaotic decomposition of the sacred writings of a Mongol people lost or dispersed in the enormous Russian plain after two centuries of triumphal invasion—and I wrapped myself in it right over my chemise.

I threw all the articles of clothing that I had taken off onto the Turkish divan up against the southwest wall, quite close to my bed, which followed the south-north diagonal of the room to the small, three-paneled folding screen that protected its head.

Then I saw the remains of my lunch on the chair.

"Who knows, she may get the idea to come looking for it," I said to myself, and, to avoid such an importunate eventuality, I carried the plate into the corridor, where I put it on the ground to the right of my door.

Back in my room, I put some sheets of paper back in order that were drooping off the writing table. This was a useful precaution, for being in the full airflow between the open windows, this table was really not a very secure place for the lyrical expansions entrusted to those pages.

"I'll burn all that, no doubt," I thought almost out loud. "They're just silly things, written by someone who doesn't know anything."

The sheets of paper disappeared into the only drawer in the table, and I went back to the bed.

I owe you, my readers, this further detail: in my bedroom, as in the room of every Russian girl of good, traditional upbringing, there was no mirror, for it was generally agreed by us that a young girl of proper habits should not be concerned about being beautiful. To be sure, very near my icons there was a small dressing table with a modest white curtain that hid the small objects indispensable to the hygiene of the body and the hair, but the mirror, symbol of great liberties, would make its appearance there only on the day of my betrothal. For the moment, its place was marked by a nail in the slender board that supported the curtain at a considerable height above the table. From this nail I had hung, on the day of St. Ivan-of-the-Waters, a crown of wildflowers. Its red and gold ribbon was still there, along with some dry stalks.

Before stretching out, I let down my long, honey-blond hair and I made this last reflection: "It will be necessary to sleep very deeply to be well awake tonight . . . at one o'clock."

These last three words joined themselves to my sentence as if independent of me, and I repeated them quite strongly: "Yes, at one o'clock."

Up there, I abandoned myself to the eider down.

In my experience, one always dreams when one sleeps, but the memory doesn't always keep the tableaux and the scenes that present themselves to our spirit, if no analogous impression from outside comes to receive and translate the fantastic content of the dream into terms of real (physical) possibility.

If we could retain every dream every time, our life would be infinitely richer, for our inner being, liberated from the prison and the skepticism of the body during sleep, would bring to our intellect a field of observations and of knowledge immensely useful for the understanding of the Unknown, that is to say of this cosmic domain where forces are beings and phenomena the plastic effects of a divine game, at the same time similar to and opposed to what commonly happens before our eyes . . .

On this day of my consecration to the tragic ghost of "Evil," a very special circumstance, and one that you shall know soon enough, allowed me to remember this astonishing dream:

First I saw a field where only wild grass grew with, here and there, some occasional little piles of sand that the sun, excessively ardent, tinted a brilliant yellow, with an unsupportable glare.

In the middle of this field a brook formed little by little, and I had the impression, although I was still not sure, of finding myself on a sort of ship that with difficulty made a passage through the humid sand of the two banks.

Because of the effort I made to explain to myself the curious situation of the ship in the narrow brook, the latter widened itself, rapidly and enormously, and all of a sudden an energetic movement precipitated the ship into a bay that opened widely upon an intensely blue horizon.

The sailors and the few other passengers on my ship began to shout with joy, and at the precise moment when I asked myself why they were feeling so happy, I saw, at some height above the horizon and right in front of us, a shining emerald disc.

I didn't have time to ask myself what it was, because the disc had already taken on the appearance of a clock, with the twelve numbers marked in sparkling gold.

The "1," quite particularly, was vibrating as if full of ardent life. It was placed to the left of the "12," which meant that this clock went in the opposite direction to our own. I fixed all my attention upon this strange "1," and it seemed to me that a red thread left it and twisted itself in zigzags and bizarre spirals around the numbers.

But no sooner had I become curious about following this thread to distinguish its different contortions than the dark shadow of an immense finger put itself through the disc, as if to indicate only the "1."

There was in the imperious will of this finger a formal prohibition against seeing the rest.

"At one o'clock," I shouted.

And this cry woke me up.

How can I tell you, without offending you, about the situation, as unexpected as it was heartrending, in which I found myself?

The two panels of my wide dressing gown hung over the

two sides of the bed, like wounded wings. My chemise was pushed up to my throat, and my young girl's belly was offered in all its nakedness to the gaze of a young man who held himself in quite an awkward position on the chair, to my right, where, an hour or two before, the plate had been deposited with the milk and the bread.

I immediately recognized the young Wassilkowsky, Misha, and trembling with shame I jumped down from the bed and ran toward the windows, tightly wrapping the dressing gown around my body.

"What right do you have to come in here?" I cried, beside myself. "Who allowed you to come into my bedroom?"

Misha didn't move. He had a stupid expression and all his wide face, under the disordered locks of his too-blond hair, reflected bewilderment, the absence of all thought. He took a large, white handkerchief from the pocket of his jacket and he pressed his right hand with it.

"Get out of here . . . immediately . . . now!" I said, exasperated. "If you don't move, I'll call everybody, the whole family, the whole household."

Misha got up with some trouble. Having regained his balance, but with his right hand still wrapped in the handkerchief, he placed himself in the middle of the room and mumbled, while smiling foolishly:

"I don't know what is frightening you so much. I haven't

done anything wrong. I only came in here by chance."

"By chance? Do you enter by chance into a bedroom that is not yours? Get out, get out, or I'll call the maid."

This precise threat no doubt brought him back to reality. He took his hand out of the handkerchief, which he put back into his pocket, not however without giving it a guilty glance.

I too looked at the handkerchief, and there I saw, to my shock, some red stains . . . One would have had to say that it was blood.

"Have you hurt yourself?" I asked.

"It's nothing," he said, "the handkerchief was already like that before. I didn't do anything, I assure you."

"How did you get the idea to come in here?" I asked again, but I was beginning to calm down.

"Quite simply," Misha said, "I was looking for the bathroom, and I saw a plate on the ground, and I entered. Besides, the door was not locked."

"Great excuse!" I answered, without however being able to keep myself from smiling, for Misha was truly droll at that moment and seemed quite naive. "We aren't in a land of savages, and a plate on the ground does not constitute an invitation to enter . . . Misha, I see that you are a little mad. Go away and don't tell anyone that you came here."

What happened to him then, I couldn't tell you. He threw himself upon me like a crazy person, and in my absolute virgin's bedroom there was a horrible scene: a body too weak to defend itself in the furious embrace of a male running wild.

My light clothing was, of course, a very bad protection against the impetuous heat of this boy of twenty-four years, and I remember very well the sensation, at first repugnant then suddenly bizarrely fascinating, that I felt in my hips at first, and then in my neck and down my back.

My resistance quickly weakened, and Misha, who realized it right away, applied his thick and humid lips to my half-opened mouth with brutality.

His tongue searched for mine, found it, and pressed itself there strongly.

"Oh! Horror!" I cried, turning away and pushing my aggressor away violently. "You're a monster! Go away!"

Misha had me by the waist, with his two arms locked together.

"Oh! No!" he said. "Now I won't go away. Besides, you're mine. I've conquered you. You belong to me."

"Monster! Monster!" I howled. "You stole my kiss. A kiss that does not belong to you. I don't belong to you, but to someone else, to an immense being beside whom you are nothing."

There was then a fantastic anger in Misha's vigorous hands and in his whole body. His small gray eyes became almost beautiful with rage. He stiffened for a moment, digging his fingernails into my skin through the fabric of the dressing gown, but he quickly cried out, triumphant: "In any case, this somebody, to whom you pretend to belong, has not known how to make himself your master!"

What did that mean?

Misha let go of me like a conqueror who knows himself victorious, and after having taken a few steps in the room, he took a chair near the writing table and sat tranquilly.

As for myself, I remained standing like a condemned person in the middle of the room.

"My lands, my lands are flooded!" I heard in a weeping voice.

Misha broke the silence first.

"Xenia," he said in a sweeter voice, "come sit there, at your place in front of your desk. The table will be an effective partition between the two of us, and you'll be able to explain yourself at your ease."

Mechanically, I obeyed. I went to sit down in front of Misha, and I placed my two hands on the granite paperweight. One has a need to touch something solid when one is troubled.

"Explain yourself," Misha ordered.

I looked at him without surprise, as if internally I recognized his right to take this tone of authority with me.

At the same time I said to him: "I have nothing to explain to you, it is you who owe me excuses."

Misha's expression was magnificent.

"Ah!" he said, from the height of his grandeur. "I see that you are forgetting that the Wassilkowskys come from proud and free Don Cossacks and that they do not allow anyone to dispute their prize . . . I affirm my right where I place myself."

"If you imagine that you have a right to me, you are mistaken," I said hollowly.

"I'm not asking for your opinion about the above," Misha answered. "What is important for me to know is the name and the place of residence of this other, of this immense being of whom you have just spoken with so much pathetic emphasis."

A wounding sarcasm underlined these words. The blood rushed to my head, my ears buzzed, tears obstructed my view.

"His name cannot be pronounced," I said.

"Ah! I assure you!" Under the look that Misha shot at me then, this determined man who peered into the depths of my being, I felt more naked, more abandoned than I had earlier, when I was stretched out on the bed with my dressing gown open.

It lasted only a second. Misha leaned back on the back of his chair and said: "You won't tell me, but I'll learn it myself. So much the worse for you, I've made up my mind . . ."

With that, he rose and left the room . . .

The door opened and closed without a sound.

THE TEST

I felt bruised, offended, dirtied by this brutal intrusion into my soul, accustomed to the sublime regions, by the insolent man who had just stolen my virginity, as if that were his right, as if I were nothing more than a piece of land, a prairie or a seashore, where the male can come and give orders according to his good pleasure.

I did not know exactly what he had done. I didn't find out until later and under circumstances that I shall relate further on, but just the fact of having been wrapped in his arms and having felt a thrill—even if it was only for a moment—at contact with his heated body, constituted a definite fall in my eyes.

I tell you sincerely: I felt that all that was my fault, and I burned with shame because of it.

Misha having left, I remained in front of my writing table, my hands pressed against the paperweight. I didn't feel that I had a right to move, nor to take the least action. Can one have any will when one feels herself unworthy of living?

And before me the place of my misdeed took on the aspect of a bitter accusation.

"I won't be able to use that bed anymore," I thought. "Each time I lie down on it I'll see my nakedness displayed before the eyes of Misha. I'll no longer be able to touch the chair where he sat, while I slept. I won't be able to open or close my door, because I'll never forget that the plate left by me at my threshold served him for an invitation, a temptation . . . and the middle of my room, where he seized me to violate me, will always seem to me to be burning with fire.

"A place of perdition, see what my bedroom has become!"

Dusk does not last long in the narrow valleys of the Caucasus, and when night falls, the temperature drops brusquely.

A blast of air, which seemed glacial to me, suddenly entered into my bedroom through the west windows. It tore away my sad reflections.

"I need to get dressed right away," I said to myself.

I took from the chest of drawers some austere undergarments and the most somber dress, and I slowly got dressed again. My arms were heavy, and my fingers obeyed me poorly.

I redid my hair and fixed it around my head, in the style of the country.

I also chose a shawl of wool from the Urals, black, with gray stripes.

"It's not the way I wanted to present myself to my sublime fiancé of the forest," I thought melancholically, "but it's impossible for me to lie: I can't dress gaily, when my soul is dispirited."

I needed to get some shoes on, too. I put on long black stockings and high shoes that came up to my calves.

"I'm in mourning, this way. Will he accept me just the same?"

Then there came to me a sort of childish caprice: I went to the little dressing table, and I took the crown of dry stalks from its nail, tied on the day of Saint Ivan-of-the-Waters, with the ribbon of symbolic colors: red and gold.

"This will be my guilty fiancée's crown," I said to myself. "I must see how it looks."

You will remember that there was no mirror in my bedroom. To judge the effect of the dry crown on my blond head, I had recourse to my customary system, also well known to all pensioners and novices in convents: I went to the window, and I looked in the glass of the open pane.

The improvised mirror returned to me the incomplete reflection of a sorrowful face with eyes deeply accentuated. The stalks on my head blended in with my tresses, and only the red and gold ribbon stood out in the shadow, like a fleeting flame.

"His clock had this red!"

This thought pierced my spirit like a bolt of lightning, and I saw again, I really saw again, with my eyes open, but without any precise localization, the strange clock of my dream, at the moment of Misha's unspeakable act.

"Take some paper and some colored pencils," a voice inside me said.

I went to my desk, I took a big piece of white cardboard, and I set down within easy reach a set of red, blue, yellow, white, and black pencils.

I remained standing.

"Draw a perfect circle," the voice ordered me.

I've never been very good at drawing, but the circle that I drew then, freehand, was truly almost regular. Between the east and north points, only, the line trembled a little, but the voice said to me: "Do not correct anything . . . Now, put in the hours."

I began: "12" at the north point, "1" to its left, then, following this same direction and at equal intervals: "2," "3," "4," "5," "6," "7," "8," "9," "10," "11."

"Write '2' above the '11,' outside of the circle."

I obeyed.

"Write '3' above the '12,' outside of the circle."

I did it.

"Place '5' above the '1,' outside of the circle."*

That was done also.

"From the new '2' to the new '5,' draw a curve parallel to the circle . . . Write as a title, 'My New Formulation' . . . Write in the margin, 'the total value of the intermediate hours is 51, or 9.' This is the symbolic number of the ERA that I combat, for it is the one that DEPRIVES ME OF MY BODY."

I was applying myself to writing all that in my best handwriting when I heard, no longer inside me but outside, and as if secretly, this sentence, which filled me with fear:

"I need a woman and a man, to be reborn from the two."

"Is it necessary to write that, too?" I asked.

"Write it in red and let a drop of your blood fall on the fifth word."†

I took the red pencil and I wrote: "I need a woman and a man, to be reborn from the two."

The drop of blood, from where should I take it? . . . Ah!

---

*[The instructions in this chapter do not produce the same drawing as the printed figure described in Naglowska's preface. The inconsistencies are not resolved by her statement in the preface that "1 = 5." For a more detailed analysis, see appendix B. —*Trans.*]

†[In French, the fifth word is "femme" (woman). —*Trans.*]

Misha's handkerchief had some. Perhaps there is also some on the sheet.

I hurried there.

Indeed!

I heard laughing near the writing table. The laugh was sarcastic, but my body felt a thrill.

Yes, there were some red stains on my sheet. I didn't ask myself where that had come from, because all of a sudden I understood a mystery that I had known nothing about until that moment.

"Misha made my blood run to steal my virginity . . . for Him!"

Oh! What joy swept over me then! What happiness! What contentment!

"You accept me then, O Thou, Sublime Martyr! You wish my sacrifice in order to become happy again!"

I took a small cotton ball that was on the dressing table. I dampened it with fresh water, and I made it absorb the blood on the sheet. Then, back at the writing table, I let fall a drop of the water, thus reddened, upon the fifth word: woman.

I felt a marvelous serenity. Everything looked different to my eyes. Peace of soul, I knew it: neither well nor ill, but . . . everything is useful.

"Let us not lay blame for anything, but let us try to discern the deep sense and the necessary reason for each event." This sentence was carved as if by itself into my spirit, and, like a student happy to receive the lesson from her Master, I sat down.

Inspiration came to me right away. Without the least hesitation, I took the red pencil and I made the line of blood run around the hours of my drawing, which I had seen wrap itself around the numbers of my clock. The spirals and the zigzags formed of themselves with an astonishing precision.

When I had finished, there was a very strange symmetrical design on the cardboard.

The red line, having started from the "1," from the left end of the curve tying together the three numerals of the new sequence, went a little past the "11" to the right end of the curve and formed three triple spirals around the "3," the "6," and the "9" respectively. The "2," the "4," the "8," the "10" remained outside and the "5," the "7," the "1," and the "11" inside the thread, each one of these numbers occupying the center of a different angle formed by the zigzags.

The whole thing presented the appearance of a sort of star with four sharp points and two round wings. The points, however, corresponding to the numbers "1" and "11" escaped into the black curve that roofed the whole thing like a cupola.

I set myself to looking for the hidden meaning of what I had just drawn:

"The total value of the intermediate hours is '9,' he had told me.*

"The three numbers of the new sequence, 5 plus 3 plus 2, form 10. Could this be the formula: ten versus nine? . . . And if it's correct, what does that mean?"

Something extraordinary happened then, which you won't believe, undoubtedly; but, on my honor, I affirm that it is true: the blue pencil, on its own, left the little leather box that held it along with the other colored pencils and placed itself vertically on the number "11," exactly between the two lines that composed it.

With an extreme rapidity, and always in the vertical position, it threw itself through the design, from the "11" to the "2," from the "2" to the "10" to the "4," from the "4" to the "8," and from there to the "6."†

---

*[54 = 9. This is only true if we consider the nonintermediate numbers to be "2," "4," "8," and "10." The sum of the twelve hours, which is also the number of cards in a tarot deck, is 78 (= 15, = 6). Twelve must therefore be included in the "intermediate hours," although it is not mentioned above. —*Trans.*]

†[The blue line agrees with the printed figure, making it likely that the same design is intended. To the red line we must add a line "3" - "9," and correct the "9" - "6" to "9" - "5" - "7" - "6." It appears that the "1 - 3 - 2" sequence written above the outer circle should be "5 - 3 - 2," so the printed figure is not completely correct, either. —*Trans.*]

On the "6" he stopped for a moment, and, bathed in perspiration, for such was my anguish, I guessed this: the "6," in its red triple enclosure, is the emblem of an organ, hidden within my body, and into which my Master wishes to penetrate.

Why?

The blue pencil took up its course, rushing from the "6" to the "7," from the "7" to the "5" to the "9," from the "9" to the "3," from the "3" to the "11," from the "11" to the "1," and darted like a swallow through the "12" and between the "3" and the "2" of the new formation, which shone then like diamonds.*

An odor spread itself around me, and I heard far off the fall of my pencil to the floor.

"I need a woman and a man," the mysterious voice said, "in order to reconquer the SIX."

Then, in the space between my eyes and the drawing, I saw the image of an egg form in luminous lines, pierced on the left, from whence an electric spark took off in a northeast direction, which left behind it a trace of vibrant gold.

"Ah! So that's why!" I said, when the image had disappeared. "In the dark prison of my body, the tortured Being

---

*[These instructions correct the deficiencies of the original red-line instructions, but they should have been done in red, rather than in blue. —*Trans.*]

will again find the strength that he needs to liberate . . . He will teach me Himself what I must do . . ."

I rested my elbows on the table, and put my forehead in my palms. All thought fled from my spirit, and I was plunged into a deep void . . .

And while I stayed thus, immobile and inert, the magical night of the Caucasus made its vivifying influence swirl around me.

JOY ON THE PLAIN

W hen I came back from my drowsiness the darkness was almost complete, and it was cool in the
room.

My first care was to see what time it was.

I gropingly found the box of matches in the usual place
between the ink pot and the vase containing the sand that I
used to dry the written pages, and I lit the two wax candles
that protruded like small, white, tepid columns from massive
silver candlesticks above the trinkets and photos arranged on
the table.

It was nine o'clock.

The yellowish light that spread out in a short radius
around the trembling little flames made fairylike shadows,
full of mystery, in the rest of the room.

"Oh! Come into the shadow of my room," I said, half
whispering.

"Come close to your fiancée, who adores you and believes you.

"Tell her what she doesn't know, and what it pleases you that she should know.

"So that, victorious and from now on without stain,

"You may show your disc and pronounce your faith.

"Behold: in sign of love, I accept the hard cross."*

The sweet music that I heard then seemed to me to be an answer to my evocation.

I abandoned myself to its lulling rhythm, and little by little my thought mingled with the charming melody, which languishing arpeggios enveloped and caressed like a crowd of amorous echoes.

"Oh! Come into the shadow of my room," this music repeated on notes sometimes shrill, sometimes grave. "Come to teach me what I don't know and what you wish that I should know. Behold: I am yours, and my whole being promises obedience."

"This music wasn't an answer then," I said to myself.

"She promises obedience," an almost-human voice said then.

It seemed to me that it came from the east windows. I turned in that direction and was astonished to see that there

---

*[In the original, these six lines make three rhymed couplets. —*Trans.*]

was light outside, a light that seemed to come from the ground floor.

I went to assure myself of it from closer up and, indeed, I saw when I leaned out the window that the three bay windows of the ballroom, of which I've already spoken above, were lit up as on the days of the great feasts.

"It's true, there's a reception this evening, Niania told me that. They are all gathered together down there no doubt and will dance and sing until late at night. But then, what should I do? It will be necessary at the same time that I get on my way immediately after midnight, to arrive at the big oak at one o'clock. The danger of getting caught will be great."

A strange idea, which was a wish rather than a thought, took hold of me then.

"I'll go dance with them," I said to myself, "and, at midnight, I'll take Misha with me."

I felt as if electrified by this decision.

"Yes, it's exactly what I need to do . . . Besides, He needs a woman and a man . . . Misha . . . since he's the one who started the . . . job . . . And above all, to decide nothing in advance, to let myself act, calmly, passively."

"She promises passivity," said the voice from earlier.

I assure you, I was afraid, but the idea that Misha would be with me at night, at one o'clock, reassured me.

"Who is it who speaks to me?" I asked.

It was the music, taken up again at that moment that answered me.

Happily! For it frightened me less than the mysteriously human speech.

I made out the following:

"... He, who has for long called you in the woods

"He, who searches in vain for roses on the stems

"Of this living plant, with immortal sap.

"To have you, at last, for me, I wish, I demand."*

"A plant? What plant?" I said, astonished. "Misha would perhaps understand these strange expressions better than I ... and now that I think about it, it would be useful to write all this down."

My readers, I tell you all these things exactly the way they happened.

You may find some incoherence there and, often, a lack of logical sequence, but it would be false on my part to want to satisfy your literary customs to the detriment of truth.

My care, in writing this book, is to bring you face to face with a mystery that it is not possible to know through the forms of discursive mentality, in vogue, alas, for too long.

The mystery that I wish to unveil for you belongs to life, and consequently it is only through the essentially chaotic

---

*[In the original, these lines form a quatrain rhymed ABAB. —*Trans.*]

forms of the latter that I must struggle to carve out a passage for you to the Root of Eternal Things.

Have patience then and follow me.

I returned to the table and, on the same sheet of cardboard that already had the magical design and the inscriptions that you know about, I wrote in cramped characters the evocation that I had pronounced when I came out of my daze, and the answer of the Unknown, which you have just read.

Having done this, I hesitated a moment, then, I added in larger letters: "I promise obedience, passivity, and . . . ?"

There are always three things in His sentences. What more must I promise?

A voice, spread though all my room, answered:

"Courage."

I wrote this word too, and at the moment when I traced the last letter "e," a bluish light crossed the room from west to east, in sharp zigzags.

An odor of sulfur followed, like a prolonging of the light, in the same direction.

"It is done," I told myself. "Now I can go downstairs."

I lit a small, special candle, surrounded, over a metal plate, by a sort of protective grillwork, and I went into the linen room, which was located in the same corridor, just across from my bedroom.

In this large, square room, I opened the two panels of

a large armoire, full of rich garments, and I chose, after an attentive examination, a dress of white silk decorated with pink and blue flowers embroidered by hand.

Then, from an oak chest of drawers, I took a chemise and a petticoat of fine Russian cloth, decorated with subtle lace work, a small, white satin corset, and a pair of very sheer stockings.

I deposited all of that in good order onto the sofa, placed in the middle of the room, and went on to the selection of some shoes.

There was a whole row of them in the bottom of the armoire: high shoes, small, polished boots, buskins, shoes without tops.

I took, as you would expect, some dancing shoes, pink with large, golden buckles. I put them on the floor in front of the sofa.

"I need some artificial flowers and some jewelry," I said to myself, "for I want to be beautiful, more beautiful than all the others."

There was, in a ragbag beside the armoire, a little chest covered in fine, gray leather. My initials shone in golden letters on its cover. I opened it by means of a small key, which I took from its hiding place in the bottom of the ragbag, and I made my choice: two beautiful tea roses, surrounded by their silky, velvet foliage, and a little, golden necklace, worked in Russian

style, with a big medallion strewn with pearls and small diamonds with a very pure fire. In the center of the medallion
there was a rooster, formed of rubies from our mountains: the
red cock of Georgia.

"That should be enough to turn Misha's head," I thought
maliciously. "It will be necessary for him to obey me without
any argument."

I proceeded to my toilette. First of all, I hastily took off
everything that I had on, and, completely nude, I made a bun-
dle of those sad clothes. Without another thought, I stuffed it
into the bottom of the armoire . . .

"It's finished," I said out loud. "The sadness and the peni-
tence are over. Now, I am light and I'm going to the ball to
celebrate my joy."

I came back to the sofa. I sat down beside the luxurious
vestments that were laid out there, and I started to pull the
stockings on.

It was the first time in my life that I had taken real joy in
the detailed operation that would make me beautiful.

With my white stockings well pulled up, I took pleasure
in noticing the elegant curve of my calves and the exceptional
delicacy of my ankles.

"Misha knows them already," I thought, smiling.

There was no longer any trace of shame in me, and it was
as if I had never had any . . .

Now, after the experience that I have acquired, thanks to the mystery of liberation—which you will know when you have read this book to the end—I can positively affirm that it was only at that moment that I began to become pure, that is to say, exempt from artificial mental constructs. For only from that moment, modesty, which is a lie in every woman, had ceased to hold me in its chains.

That will shock you, perhaps, but it is necessary that I establish here this truth: liberation from the lie of modesty, beyond its occult value, also has practical usefulness because it makes the woman free from the perversity of the man.

Indeed, frankness with respect to herself, in sexual matters, creates in the woman a simplicity of attitude that keeps the degenerate man away (he who has need of sordid and hidden [forbidden] procedures to satisfy himself).

Only the man whose sexual force is healthy approaches the woman who has simplicity of attitude (pure, in the sense understood here), and what results from it is always holy: within the order of terrestrial things, that is to say, mortal ones, for their inferiors, and within the order of divine things, that is to say, immortal ones, for their superiors.

This is an ancient truth. It is even the most ancient. But

humans, who have neglected—alas, for too long—divine problems in order to occupy themselves only with social questions and proprieties (which are always in contradiction with the former) have completely forgotten it.

Society has established laws and customs that hinder Life from developing itself harmoniously, and that is why many very natural things have become mysteries to it.

But Truth is now coming back into the light, because its hour has sounded . . .

As I entered the packed ballroom, I was radiant with joy in my luminous outfit, with its springtime nuances, the tea roses pinned above the neckline where the beginning of my heavy tresses fell, like two large boas down to my knees and surrounding my neck with a soft caress.

They were listening with sincere attention to a classical piece, played on the piano by a quite pretty and elegant young woman.

The guests were seated along the whole length of the walls, on the white and gold chairs that made up, as you know, the room's only furniture.

All the family members were there, the permanent residents and the visitors come for the evening: the Wassilkowskys and some other neighbors.

Each one was surprised to see me enter so unexpectedly,

and in the looks that they raised in my direction it was easy to read their admiration.

One of my aunts, meanwhile, made a sign to me to not disturb the group, and, obeying, I sat down on the first free chair, very near the door where I had entered.

It was at that moment that I saw Misha.

He was standing near one of the windows that looked out to the northeast and seemed to be the only one indifferent to the music.

He looked at me as one waking up from a terrible inquietude, and his eyes said to me: "Later."

I supported his gaze with a playful indifference, and that visibly bothered him. The resolution that he had at that moment certainly increased because of it.

The young woman, pretty and elegant, suddenly stopped her playing on a chord that she struck noisily.

She rose and said:

"I've forgotten the rest, I haven't practiced for a long time."

Everyone crowded around her, and there was a general brouhaha of compliments and congratulations to her.

Misha approached me:

"What have you been doing all this time?" he asked, with the imperious tone of a commanding officer.

"I was in my room," I answered.

"I know very well that you haven't left it," he said, "but what were you doing?"

I found no answer, for, indeed, what had I been doing there?

"You don't want to answer?" Misha murmured between his teeth.

"Yes and no," I said, laughing.

"What does that mean: yes and no? Do you want to answer me, or don't you?"

"I would really like to," I said. "Look, I really and truly do, but I don't know how to explain it to you."

"Then it was a quite complicated task," Misha said, with a bitter fold at the corner of his mouth. "It's strange how women always have to make things mysterious. . . . But with me you'll have to lose this habit."

"Look, Misha, your nervousness is exaggerated, to say the least."

"Ah! You think so!" he said.

He looked through me.

Our conversation ended there, for a radiant officer approached us and said to Misha:

"Have you engaged your lady for the contra dance?"

Without hesitating, Misha seized my arm, passed it under his, and said: "Obviously."

"Ah! Pardon me!" the officer said. "I intended to

invite mademoiselle, but since you have preceded me . . ."

He then bowed politely and glided away.

I stayed on Misha's arm. Then my mother came through the crowd. She stopped near us, wanted to say something to me, but, after a second of reflection and a kind smile in the direction of Misha, she in turn went away.

"What is my mother thinking at this moment?" I said to Misha. "What do you think?"

"That makes no difference to me," the young man answered.

He now had the expression of a conqueror, and I won't hide from you that it gave me pleasure.

"Let's dance," he said to me, "and we'll be better than all of them. Do you know how to dance the Cossack gallop?"

"Yes," was my answer.

"Great! The two of us, soon!"

He led me, always giving me his arm, into the corner between the two rows of windows. You will not have forgotten that this was the north point of the house. He took two chairs, which he placed one beside the other, and asked me to sit down.

When the two of us were installed there, and while the agitation continued around us, for the gentlemen invited their ladies and the old people arranged themselves in the corners of the hall so as to leave as much room as possible for the dancers, Misha had this conversation with me:

"Listen, Xenia, you have to stop playing the innocent. You no doubt understand that I have chosen you to guard you. I'll fight harshly for you with any competitor. So if you don't want there to be a tragedy here, tell me immediately who you are in love with, so that I can get him out of my hair as soon as possible."

Ah! Woman's malice is full of resources!

"Misha," I answered, "if you want to know everything, I invite you to follow me tonight, immediately after midnight, into the forest. Are you familiar with the old, giant oak?"

"Yes," Misha said, white as a sheet. "And there?"

"And there you shall know everything."

"He's waiting for you down there?"

"Yes, tonight, at one o'clock."

Misha remained silent. He frowned fiercely and clenched his fists.

"Very well," he said, "I'll bring my big Cossack saber. As a matter of fact, I sharpened it well this morning."

We stayed awhile longer in the north corner of the hall, but we didn't say anything more.

Misha appeared to be hatching a plan, and, to be sure, I had no interest in turning his thought away from the grass around the giant oak, where he was imagining meeting a flesh-and-blood rival like himself.

We didn't dance, either one of us, and to the gentlemen who came to invite me, I invariably answered: "I'm not feeling up to it today. It will be for another time."

The members of my family deduced, naturally, the most ordinary thing from my conduct, which was also, from their point of view, the best: that Misha and I were preparing an engagement.

Suddenly Misha shivered.

"There is a strange draft of air there," he said.

He rose and closed the nearest windows, to the right and left of our two chairs.

He went back to his place, and got up again.

"The strange thing," he said, "is that the wind is coming from below. It's not winter, though. My feet are frozen. Come out to the balcony, walking a little will do us good."

"We'll have to pass in front of all the old ladies," I observed, "and disturb the dancers."

"We are not in Paris or Petersburg," Misha answered, "we'll have to make the best of it."

He opened the window, which he had just closed, placed one of our chairs in front of the windowsill to serve as a step ladder, and asked me in a cross tone: "Would you be afraid of scandalizing everyone by using this make-shift ladder? Come, Xenia, don't hesitate and hell with the public."

"I don't need a very great effort for such a simple act," I said, laughing, and, without leaning on the hand that he offered, I jumped onto the chair, from the chair to the windowsill, and from there to the flagstones of the balcony. All of that in less time than it takes to write it.

Misha followed me in a single stride.

The night was very dark. No moon, and myriad stars, large and scintillating, seemed to aim infinite, anguished looks at the earth.

The air was cool and alive.

"Ah! It's better here," Misha said, inhaling the night breeze deeply. "What time is it?"

He pulled his watch from its pocket.

"Eleven o'clock."

He shivered nervously.

"It's almost time to begin our preparations," he said.

He took a few steps along the wall, while, immobile, I contemplated the splendid depths of the sky. These majestic lines of our great poet Apouchtine came to my mind:

> *The august ranges*
> *Sleep in the night.*
> *The valleys wind*
> *Without a sound.*

The forests keep silent,
The pools are sweet.
The awful hurt
Will end . . . wait!*

"Yes, indeed," I thought, "everything ends and everything begins on time, at the minute ordered beforehand. The essential thing, in order to not oppose the unknown will, is to remain calm and passive under all circumstances. No personal desires, above all."

Misha came back toward me.

"What are you thinking about?" he asked, pressing my two arms in his strong hands. "Xenia, I want you to love me. Me. Not the other."

I tightened my lips. No answer came to my spirit. Misha interpreted my silence in his favor, no doubt, though it

---

*[In French these two quatrains are rhymed ABAB. They have every appearance of having been written in French originally, not translated from Russian. Although there was a person with the name Apouchtine who wrote words for some music of Tchaikovsky, the name does not appear on any list of Russian poets, great or otherwise, that I could find. I believe that Apouchtine is one of Naglowska's many pseudonyms. In its style and the kinds of rhyme used, the poem is very much like others that Naglowska wrote and signed with her own name. A slightly different version of this poem (with "Your awful hurt" instead of "The awful hurt") had already been published in the first number of *La Flèche,* also credited to "Apouchtine." —*Trans.*]

had a quite different cause, and drawing me passionately against his wide chest, he deposited an ardent kiss over my right eye.

"I love your eyes," he said, and a moment later: "the other does not love you, I'm sure, I'll prove it to you."

"You'll know everything at one o'clock," I said, but my voice choked in my throat.

"Yes, yes, I'll know everything, and I'll fight hard, if it's necessary," Misha said, "because I want you."

He looked at me again and again, then he detached himself from me with a great effort and shivered from head to foot.

"Are you bringing a cloak?" he suddenly asked. "You'll also need some more solid shoes."

"You're right," I said. "I'll go and get what I need soon enough. The grass is damp at night."

"No, go right away. I'll be here when you come back."

He cast a worried look around.

"We have to go down by this ladder, right?" he asked, pointing to the iron ladder, which led from the balcony into the courtyard of the peacocks and geese.

"Yes."

"Alright! Go! We'll meet in the courtyard, at the foot of the ladder. Here would not be prudent . . . I have something to get, too, before we leave."

His eyes shone with an evil gleam.

Poor Misha! He was thinking, no doubt, about his saber.

When I came back—perhaps a half hour later, for I had to go all the way around the house, by the southeast rooms, the hall, the interior stairway and, at last the corridor off which my room was located—Misha stood a few steps away from the iron ladder, protected from the light that came from the windows of the ballroom.

The silence was profound, for the dancers and all the guests and the members of the family had gone into the dining room, where a copious, Russian-style supper held all their attention.

Under the enigmatic glimmer of the stars, strong in these southern regions, where the sky seems low and massive, the faint silhouette of the snowy peaks could be seen as imprecise scallops and seemed to invite the spirit on a mysterious voyage into unknown depths.

The darker stains of the thickly forested valleys had a sinister aspect, and the nervous fear that they inspired was a powerful stimulant for a brave soul.

A cold breeze passed through. I felt that it contained a thought and a will that would soon be revealed to me.

I went down slowly, placing my feet, shod in small, polished shoes, carefully on the narrow steps of the iron ladder.

I looked at Misha, who in the darkness was giving himself to an exercise that was, to say the least, bizarre: he had his big Cossack saber in his right hand, and with this weapon, weakly illuminated at moments, he was tracing large circles in the air, which he then cut from top to bottom and from left to right, straight in front of him. On the ground, at a meter or two from him, a lantern was deposited, which projected a red glow through its panes.

I stopped on the last step of the ladder, to watch what Misha was doing.

My eyes, which had in the meantime grown used to the dark, permitted me to pick out the young man's face: he looked inspired, and unintelligible sounds came from his half-open lips: Ho! Hey! Ho! Hey! Ha! And still other syllables that I couldn't pick out.

With an instinctive gesture, I pulled the folds of the large cloak that I had thrown over my shoulders to keep away the night's cold and to cover my pale dress. I wouldn't for anything in the world have wanted to draw Misha's attention at that moment, or to disturb him in his strange operation, for it was obvious to me that he had already—oh! to my great joy!—come under the influence of my mysterious Master. *I need a man and a woman,* he had said.

Misha took a step forward and because of it found himself lightly illuminated.

I saw then that he wore all the Cossack equipment: the long caftan trimmed with gray lamb's wool, a cap of the same fur, and numerous daggers stuck into his leather belt. His high boots reached above his knees. He was impressive, and I couldn't keep from feeling a lively admiration for him.

"Forty-one," he said, in an atonal voice, "forty-one is the number of the voyage, completed from the *eleven* to the *six*. It is the number of the first consecration, after the descent to the center of the egg."*

He became silent for an instant, caught his breath, and continued like a lesson learned by heart, which one mumbles again in order not to forget it:

"Forty-one is the number of the threshold attained. It is the addition: 11 plus 2, plus 10, plus 4, plus 8, plus 6. At this threshold one dies or one goes on in the ascension . . . Now, it's a matter of realizing, on the way up, 7 plus 5, plus 9, plus 3, plus 11, plus 1, or 36 all together[†] . . . Thirty-six plus 41 make 77, that is why the number 77 is that of liberation . . . It is the second consecration, that of the Master in the male . . . It is also the second 5 . . . the 5 . . . the *star* of the Other Shore . . ."

---

*[This agrees with the path of the darker line on the Aum Clock design at the front of the book. —*Trans.*]

†[This is also in agreement with the illustration and represents the path of the lighter line. — *Trans.*]

Misha took three more steps forward, with the stiff gait of a sleepwalker, and pronounced in a terribly strong voice, holding his saber *en garde:*

"I promise you and I invite you to ascend through me from the *Six* to the *One,* that is from 41 to 77 . . ."

My readers, you are by now used to the extravagances of this tale, so I can calmly tell you, and without useless excuses, that at the moment when Misha pronounced the word "seventy and seven" (for he did not say it in the usual way), a blue flame fell upon the point of his saber and there disappeared, like a serpent into the earth.

Very near me, a hushed voice murmured:

"Ask him three questions, and do not forget his answers. Do it quickly, for he has little time available to you."

I was searching for a question to ask, when all of a sudden, and as if in spite of me, I said:

"Why is it necessary to combat the *nine?*"

"That's it," whispered the breeze, which redoubled at that instant.

Misha, still like an automaton, answered:

"The *nine* is the symbol of the *six* reversed. It is the lie that speaks the language of the true. It is My cross, perpetuated by the triumph of the Unjust."

"Ask the second question," the same hushed voice said.

This time I had a clear sensation that it came from the north.

Without reflecting, I asked:

"Who is the Unjust?"

Misha turned slowly toward me, thus presenting his face to the south, and said:

"The Unjust is he who keeps shame of life in humanity. The Unjust is he who replaces the living water of the Sea with the lie of the simulacrum. The Unjust is he who loves My cross, because it keeps Me from finishing My cycle."

"Ask the third question, and hurry, for it's late," murmured the hushed voice, this time also distinctly from the north.

I said then:

"How may we vanquish Your *cross*, Your *nine*, Your *prison*?"

I said "prison," but that astonished me enormously, and I gave all my attention to understanding the answer to this last question, which I had formulated in spite of myself, but whose importance appeared to me immediately.

Misha answered:

"One cannot vanquish the *Cross*, the *Nine*, the *Prison*, except in realizing My work, My cycle, My liberty. He who shall have accepted and liberated me will be powerful and wise, for I will be in him and he will be Me."

A violent nervous trembling then took hold of Misha. He lowered the saber and leaned on it, wobbling.

I felt permission to help him. I jumped to the ground and ran toward him. Not knowing how to keep him from falling—for, obviously, he was quite heavy for me—I pushed him against the wall, which was only a few steps away from us. He backed up right away and, having arrived near the wall, he leaned against it with visible relief.

His saber scraped in the gravel.

"Misha," I said, "have no fear, you are all right now."

He breathed deeply the cool air of the night, shivered again, and looked at me.

"There you are, Xenia," he said. "I've just had an extraordinary vision. Give me your hand, my friend, I'm beginning to understand many things."

THE CROSSING

We set out, hand in hand. Misha had said:

"Come, Xenia, it's time."

And I followed him without saying a word.

We knew the path well, he and I.

Misha held the lantern in his right hand, its red light spread a weak glow around us; and in the thick night it was as if we were going through a tunnel.

At the same time, as we advanced, the space gained closed again behind us, like a black wall.

When we arrived at the end of the great walk on the grounds that surrounded my ancestral home, after which it would be a matter of dealing with unkept paths, Misha stopped and said to me:

"Rest a little, my friend. I'll take advantage of it to tell you certain things."

The manifest change in Misha's whole attitude did not

surprise me, because I knew the reason for it, but what seemed astonishing to me was my completely new feeling with regard to my companion.

This feeling was very different from the mystical love that I had felt for the Unknown: he effaced me more in my own eyes and was spread through me, as an overwhelming influence.

When I was seated upon the trunk of an overturned pine, well wrapped in my big black cloak, elbows resting on my knees and forehead in palms, Misha, who had remained standing, said to me:

"Xenia, I know now that he who is waiting for us in the forest is neither a rival nor an adversary. He is a friend, and the teaching that He shall give us bears upon a sacred mystery. That is why it is appropriate for us to prepare in a worthy fashion for the solemn meeting."

He stopped talking and gathered himself into a deep meditation.

He was truly superb, illuminated by the red glow against the black background of the night. His eyes seemed enormous and powerful, and his tall, vigorous Cossack's stature reflected an indomitable will.

I looked at him, and I didn't think about anything. I waited for everything from him now.

"Xenia," he said at last, "have you anything to reproach me about?"

If the earth had opened and swallowed me up, if the Kasbek had bowed down in front of the sea, I would have been less shaken in my being: I, reproaching anything in this man!

In a single bound I was on my feet, with my arms around Misha's neck, like a mad woman. I pressed against his body, hard as granite, I wrapped my legs around his, I ruined my clothes in rubbing against his daggers.

From time to time, I threw my head back to see if he was smiling.

Misha allowed me to continue for a few moments. He took me into his arms then and hugged me tenderly.

I wish I could express the happiness I felt, feeling his strength and rigidity turn to tenderness for me.

I was aware, I felt the need to sacrifice myself. Oh! The voluptuousness of the sacrifice!

"You are right," Misha whispered, lightly caressing my ear with his lips, "you are right: you can't reproach me for it . . . Xenia is mine, because I have won her. Xenia belongs to no one else . . . the Other is not an enemy . . . we shall see Him soon . . . together . . . kiss me again, my little blue-bird . . . give me the kiss that I need now . . . I'm not the same person that I was this morning . . . we shall see Him together, soon."

Saying that, he lifted me like a child, without effort, as if

I had no weight, and, when my head was at the level of his, our lips united in a marvelous kiss, which seemed to unite heaven and earth.

There was no hell in that kiss, for hell had already been crossed.

Hell's kiss is humid, because it is the beginning of the great crossing of the Sea. Heaven's kiss is airy and radiant, because it is the first step taken on the new shore.

But one does not cross over the Sea, if one does not reach the limit of the first land . . . and the man will not pass over the region of the waves, if the waves do not make way for him. The woman is the wave and the man is the land.

"Yes, I'm yours, Misha, yours alone . . ."

I was elated and without strength.

Misha plunged a caressing look into my eyes and said to me:

"It's true."

He placed another kiss on my forehead, between my eyebrows, a kiss charged with thoughts, and, slowly, as if I were a fragile and precious object, he put me back on the trunk of the pine.

"Now, rest peacefully and don't move, no matter what happens. What I have to do now is for me and because of me. Don't be concerned, stay completely calm."

Without effort, I obeyed. I found it sweet to obey him. I crossed my hands on my knees and I waited.

Misha backed up a few steps. He extended his arms before him, presenting his palms to the sky as the priest does in front of the altar when he implores the divine powers for Christ to descend into the bread and wine of the Mystery.

He immediately brought about a concentration of spirit and of formidable forces.

He resembled a red statue of transparent stone. The light lost itself around him in the immense darkness, but the force that was in him seemed still more immense. It was the center that dominated the night.

Slowly, Misha turned his palms. He raised his arms to the sky and began to bend his knees to a very slow rhythm. His spine curved when his knees touched the earth, and he performed before me the solemn salute of our ancestors, his forehead in the dust of the ground.

All my being revolted at seeing him thus bowed down before me, but he had ordered me to remain immobile and I did as he had wished.

Misha rose and repeated the same salute a second time.

He straightened up immediately, regained his habitual proud posture, removed the saber from its sheath, made the steel play in the free air of the night, as if he wished to signal to some invisible witnesses that his test was finished and that a prize of liberty crowned his victory, and, addressing himself to me, he said in a clear and joyous voice:

"Xenia, my woman, my friend, my lover! As you know, I belong to the valiant race of the Don Cossacks. No one, among us, has ever bent his backbone before any power of the earth. The czar, himself, speaks to us with respect, and we go to war because we wish to. No one shall oblige us to serve the defense of a cause that displeases us. Still, today, I rolled my forehead in the dust in front of you: a woman . . . I'll explain to you now why I did it. Remember my words, for you won't understand their sense immediately . . . Something is going to happen at one o'clock tonight and then, only, the key of the mystery will be given to you . . . but I won't be there, then, to tell you this . . . So listen, and be the nocturnal witness to my oath: here, in this forest, I have said good-bye to all your sisters, to all women, in you . . . I swear on your head that henceforth no woman shall know me.

It was extraordinary: heartrending and tragic.

It seemed that, in the shadows, the leaves trembled like me and that the trees bent their large branches over me to protect me, or rather to console me.

But there was no noise in the forest, and the stars, in the black sky, were calm.

Nature accepted Misha's solemn oath.

He began to speak again:

"I repeated my salute twice," he said, "because I have learned, understood, and decided two things: it is necessary to break with woman and to thank her . . . My first salute was the sorrowful salute of the rupture, and the second the expression of my gratitude . . . Xenophonta, you are the flesh through which I have been sanctified. Before knowing you, I was just a wild beast—through you, Understanding has come to me . . . through you, because you had received it before me . . . soon I shall know why that was so . . . He, you, me? . . . the black, the white, the red? . . . I'm in a hurry to know that, but I already sense it as an immense joy . . . and I render homage to you—O Xenophonta, O blessed flesh of His desire!—for without you I would not have known how to perform the Crossing . . . Xenia, my friend, receive the sign of my gratitude."

He gathered a spray of flowers from a branch and slipped it into my bodice, between the two breasts.

"Let's get on our way," he said rapidly.

It was still a long way.

At first we followed a path on the wooded slope, where the brooks were frequent.

Hand in hand, we jumped those humid veins of the earth, and Misha said to me:

"Courage, my little Xenia, the reward awaits you."

The red light projected by our lantern accompanied us like a protective sphere. It frightened away the hungry animals that wandered in the clearings in search of prey.

Branches cracked in the darkness and I quivered in spite of myself.

Then, Misha's hand pressed my frightened fingers more strongly, and that comforted me.

But I didn't dare to speak, for I had a profound respect for the world into which his spirit had penetrated.

I invented something else to oblige him to occupy himself with me more often: even when I was not afraid, and when everything was peaceful, I shuddered just so that he would squeeze my hand.

He understood it, no doubt, for he soon said:

"Xenia, instead of growing, you are diminishing . . . but that is well . . . that must be, too . . . When we arrive at the giant oak . . . at the place where He is waiting for us . . . I'll have nothing but a small child, without understanding, with me . . . And when you no longer know anything, I'll take you in my arms . . . then you will be something that the Spirit does not fear . . ."

He said that in a muffled voice, as if to himself.

I didn't try to penetrate the meaning of his words, and I

contented myself with absorbing their flavor, as one drinks a liqueur so that it will tickle your insides.

My brain was putting itself to sleep.

We left the woods and entered into the narrow gorge, where a rapid torrent rolls its reddish waters toward the impetuous Terek.*

Long before we got there, the sonorous rippling of its foam warned us of the danger.

We approached it with careful steps, and Misha leaned over the water to see if there was a practicable crossing.

In this open place, the night was less somber, for the glow of the stars joined the scintillating reflection of the snows and ices of the surrounding summits. I spotted a slimy and rampant creature that raised its head from the water, very close to Misha's right foot.

"Watch out!" I yelled, "that thing will hurt you."

"You think so?" Misha asked, "Your courage is disappearing, then!" And he added, "But that is also right, for the flesh is fearful."

He pulled out his saber, and presented its point to the beast. Sparks flew from the steel and the animal fled, hissing.

---

*[Bearing in mind that the story is an initiatic allegory, there can be little doubt that this is a reference to "the red river of animal life" spoken of in the first two books of this series, which must be crossed for transcendence to be achieved. —*Trans.*]

Misha reflected for a moment.

"Take the lantern," he said. "I'm going to make a bridge. Otherwise we won't be able to cross."

He gathered some large stones and threw them, one by one, into the torrent.

That formed, indeed, a sort of rustic dike, against which the current dashed itself in furious bursts.

With the point of his saber, Misha assured himself of the solidity of his construction, and said:

"Do you want to go first? The bridge is narrow, there isn't room for two."

I remained perplexed.

I sensed that this question was a test. I wanted to give him the answer that he wanted, but I couldn't guess what that was.

Misha repeated his question:

"Will you go first?"

I still hesitated.

"Ah! Your will has disappeared, too!" he exclaimed, mad with joy. "Nothing left, nothing left, neither understanding nor will. That is the way you had to become."

He gathered me in his arms and crossed the stone bridge, running.

I barely had the presence of mind to hold on to the lantern, which almost got away from me.

ON THE
OTHER SHORE

On the other bank, Misha did not put me down.

He installed me comfortably on his left arm and said:

"Pass your right arm around my neck, and abandon yourself to unconsciousness. The flesh is pure, when the intellect sleeps . . . don't listen to the murmur of the night, nor feel the breath of the breeze . . . be deaf to all that happens outside . . . For now all your tests are finished . . . What the stars whisper still does not concern you . . . Be happy, your Master permits it."

I rested my head on Misha's big fur hat, and I closed my eyes.

The climb was hard on the abrupt ramp. From time to time Misha stopped and tested the ground with the point of his saber.

Stones rolled then on the rocky soil, and far off the echoes repeated the noise of their fall into the valley.

Misha climbed the slope with the firm step of a hero.

My arm was bare around his neck.

My skin warmed itself voluptuously from his warmth, and a sweet feeling of well-being spread through me.

Soon, I felt nothing but that . . .

. . . Had I slept, or been unconscious?

I heard strange, vague sounds, I felt the passage of something indefinable . . . whether it was near or very far from me, I couldn't have said . . .

A very special indolence invaded me and took away all desire to understand what was happening around me. I didn't even ask myself where I was; no curiosity impelled me to know the place where I had arrived . . .

All of a sudden, I felt a strange weight on my knees . . .

Was someone touching me? . . . Where?

The indolence took me again, I forgot my knees . . .

A little later, I opened my eyes, for a yellow light was tickling my retina . . . I saw green glows, red, blue, edged with gold.

Stars formed rapidly and disappeared quickly in fleeting circles . . .

"But what is over my eyes? What is it that glues my eyelashes?"

I tried to open my eyes, but my eyelids did not obey me.

"There is something strange over my eyes. Something rubs against my eyelashes and makes me lower my eyelids . . . And my knees, why are they so heavy? . . . Someone is holding them down with his hands . . . Who then? . . . Ah! It's undoubtedly this strange object, placed over my eyes, that keeps me from understanding . . . Someone—but who?—wants my knees to be heavy, wants them to hurt me . . . They want to keep me from extending my legs comfortably . . . And these stars, these stars, what are they doing in my eyes? . . . Stars, triangles, circles, flashes, red, green, gold . . ."

"It is the gold that predominates now," a voice near me declared.

"It is necessary to listen." I told myself. "But why are they holding my knees? That keeps me from listening."

"Spread perfumes, and sing songs of joy," ordered the same voice. "The work is accomplished and gold predominates now."

"They will sing," I thought. "It is absolutely necessary for me to listen."

Indeed, a chorus of numerous voices intoned a chant that I did not know.

"This chant gives off an aroma," I thought, "a perfume of amber and violets . . . Oh! It's beautiful!"

The chorus came nearer, no doubt, for I distinctly heard these words:

"Rejoice, O immortal hero! The hour of your crowning has sounded."

"Misha!" I said.

I don't know whether I said it out loud.

The chant continued.

"Rejoice, Mishaël, conqueror of the fire and conqueror of the waters: you have won the scepter of the earth. Nature has bowed before you and, like an impassible god you have crossed the Threshold.

"Your eyes have seen, and your ears have heard, but your flesh has remained dry.* None of your muscles has trembled and you remained intact in the middle of the waves . . . For your strength is great, O immortal one."

"Oh! Let go of my knees, I beg you!"

This time, I heard my voice.

They helped me immediately, and I took advantage of it to extend my legs voluptuously.

But then I was very cold, and I complained of it.

"Cover her," ordered the voice that seemed to command the others.

---

*[In Naglowska's writings, this phrase always means that ejaculation has been avoided. In the previous sentence, "Threshold" refers to the vaginal opening, the threshold that we all cross when we are born. —*Trans.*]

It was not the voice of Misha: it was more serious, deeper.

People were stirring around me.

Hands, full of solicitude, pressed near my head and made it take a more agreeable position.

I felt, only then, that the pallet on which I was stretched out was very hard.

The chorus took up its singing again:

"Contemplate the flesh offered in holocaust. Listen to the voice wherein is no more reasoning. Consider the voluntary offering, O powers of heaven, of the stars and of the earth, and recognize that this work is beautiful!"

Other voices, also in chorus, answered:

"We have come from far and from near. We have come from the seven regions of the air, we have witnessed the hero's test, and we declare that he has overcome."

Then the voice that commanded said:

"Mishaël, receive the sword, prize of your victory."

There were slight noises around me. They came forward, they retreated, but no one seemed to be walking: there was no sound of footsteps.

"He has seized the sword," I said all of a sudden. "Yes, they asked me that," I immediately thought. "They wanted to know if I knew it without seeing it."

And I added in a loud voice:

"Yes, Mishaël, Misha, has taken into his right hand the sword, which was offered to him."

I did not know how I had come to know that.

"Answer her," the voice ordered.

The first chorus then sang a very sweet melody. The words were approximately the following:

"Blessed be the woman, who offers herself as a narrow gorge between two mountain walls, to permit the Glorious to test in silence the real strength of his resolution.

"O all of you, O you souls near and far! Render thanks to this child: the veil, placed over her earthly eyes, did not prevent her from discerning the Truth. But, sublime, she is unaware of her own merit.

"For the wisdom of the Great Alchemist is here, constructor of Life: He pours into the woman the corrosive poison whose subtle virtue decomposes the vulgar metals, allowing naught to sink in but the transparent gold.

"Often the ground is too humid, and then the operation remains without solution. Life feels the pain of it, and one hears everywhere the cries of distress.

"The Master, in these periods, becomes the Wicked One, and humanity translates his howl of despair by cries and acts of anger. Nature becomes angry and spits muddy waters, while among men, wars and revolutions break out. When the pain is at its peak, the mother hates her son.

"But praise this child, for, through her, the Magical work has been able to be completely accomplished.

"She has loved the Master, and the Master has been able to penetrate into her, to fertilize her and fill her with the gift of Understanding.

"O Mishaël! O free warrior of the rivers, bough detached from the branch, which flowered even so, you have been able to take and leave without weakening, because you have understood that through her your soul united itself with Him.

"To Him, the Master and Architect, who built the world according to a subtle geometry, be glory and devotion!

"To Him, the Creator and Organizer of Love, supreme law of dissolution, be homage and gratitude of our hearts!

"To Mishaël and to Xenophonta, his bride, be glory, wisdom, and virtue!"

The second chorus responded:

"Yes, glory to Mishaël! And glory to his Bride! . . . Glory to the man and the woman who lent themselves to the realization of the cycle of magical love, according to the will of the Master of Life, the Wise Alchemist, who projected himself from the North to the South, but whom the reaction of the contrary forces stops at the center, to crucify Him from the East to the West.

"Glory to the Master of Life! Glory to the Crucified One,

whose two hands, detached from the wood of shame, join here in a sign of joy.

"Let us salute the Sacred Triangle, formed in this place, under the old, giant oak that guards its secret: let us salute the *Hé,* which is the call to the work, the emission of the seed, the satanic will projected into Life; let us salute the lower point of the dynamic axis, the sorrowful *Hô,* the name of the crucified flesh; and let us salute the *La* of the new formation, the point that is at the same time the flight and the return; for as it is said by those who know the keys of Wisdom, an old name pronounced by a new mouth is a new name, a rebirth."*

The chorus became quiet, and the voice that directed the ceremony said to Misha:

"Mishaël, pronounce your new name, for from now on you incarnate the freed will of the Master."

This was a solemn moment.

A striking silence reigned in the deep shadows.

Then, at the precise moment when the veil suddenly fell from my eyes, exposing my gaze to an astonishing light, Misha, in a firm voice, pronounced these three syllables: *Hé-Hô-Là.*

---

*[The three italicized vocables evidently represent the three Persons of the Trinity. Naglowska makes sure that we know that the third one is feminine by naming it with the syllable that is the feminine direct article in most Romance languages. —*Trans.*]

Then I saw my hero standing on a little hill, very close to the old, giant oak, which extended its full, heavy branches above his royal head.

Misha's face emanated a glow that agitated the whole grassy area with a strange scintillation, alternately silvery, golden, and red.

It was a light such as I had never seen in my life.

In his right hand Misha held a fiery sword, and in his left hand the golden sphere that symbolizes imperial power.

His Cossack clothes were covered by a long cloak, of which it was difficult to say whether it was of crystal or of linen.

Around the grassy area, a crowd of radiant beings, separated into two wings, to the right and to the left of Misha, vibrated like a magnetic vapor.

They were the two choruses that had sung the "glories" and the "teachings" of Wisdom . . . The perfumes and the music!

My pallet, composed of some large stones and freshly gathered boughs, was placed in the middle of the grassy area.

It was turned in such a way that my head was in the north and my feet in the south.

I had no clothes under my black cloak, thrown over my body as a covering.

I looked for the eyes of the Master of the ceremony, he who commanded the others, but I did not see him.

"Where is the Master?" I asked.

There was, in the vaporous assembly, something like a thrill of joy, and the choruses again began to sing, together, something that was completely incomprehensible to me.

Misha seemed not to concern himself with me, but I must also say that his eyes, which were nothing but light and fire, had a look that mortals do not know.

Perhaps he saw me, but differently.

. . . Later, when it was all finished, because the Dawn pointed through the thick forest and chased away the nocturnal verities, Misha, having become a Cossack again, helped me to put my clothes back on.

He brought me some strawberries from the woods and some fresh water, drawn from the nearby source.

He was happy and tranquil.

"What will you do now?" I asked him, when we were seated, one beside the other, on the humid grass, like two workers who had finished their task.

He did not answer immediately; we were in no hurry.

"What will I do?" he said at last, "I will teach you, Xenia. I'll tell you, in human speech, the celestial Truth that has been unveiled for me tonight, thanks to you . . .

"Later, much later, you will communicate this Truth to the multitudes, and the human echo will repeat it, as well as it can . . . We will celebrate a human marriage so that people will leave us in peace . . . Good morning, my fiancée," he said, smiling.

Other things combined later with this first event, which determined, forever, my spiritual orientation.

Perhaps I shall tell you about them, one day . . .

ABOUT THE NEW RELIGION

THE DOCTRINE OF THE THIRD TERM OF THE TRINITY

THE DIVINITY IS TRIPLE: THE FATHER, THE SON, AND THE MOTHER

The Father is the setting out, or the Fall, from the Origin toward the level of division and multiplicity.

The Son is nostalgia and the will to universal redemption, combated by the Adversary inherent to His nature: Satan.

The Mother is the return toward the Origin, after the definitive combat and the reconciliation in the Son of His two opposing natures: the Christic nature and the satanic nature.

The Son detaches himself from the Father and divides himself in two: He is double.

The Mother proceeds from the Father and the Son and contains both of them: She is triple.

Only the Father is homogeneous.

The three aspects of the Trinity—the Father, the Son, the Mother—are successive in time but simultaneous in their Eternal Presence in the regions that are not involved on the level of division and multiplicity.

The succession—Father, Son, Mother—is justified thus:

The Father is the Male principle, which accomplishes the act of negation of the Unique Spirit; it is love oriented toward the flesh.

The Son is the principle of the second negation, that which in the flesh rejects the flesh; it is love oriented toward the unreal, the love of the infertile heart. The Son is neither Male nor Female: he is on this side of the two divine sexes. He is, because of that, beyond sexed beings.

The Mother is the reestablishment of the Male principle in the inverse sense: She affirms the Unique Spirit, and her love, taking rise in the flesh, is oriented toward spiritual realization. She consoles and glorifies the Son, for She makes concrete the dream of sublime purity in multiple life. The Mother pacifies the combat between Christ and Satan in leading these two contrary wills onto the same path of unique ascension. The Mother proceeds from the Father and from the Son and is successive to them in temporal subordination, because negation is not converted to affirmation except by means of the second negation.

When the work of the Mother is accomplished, that of the Father recommences, for the three aspects of the Divine Trinity are repeated endlessly.

In human history, the three divine phases are reflected in the form of three types of religions, which succeed each other constantly, determining three types of civilizations, which we find in the cycle—or triangle—to which we belong in these three religion-civilizations: Judaism, Christianity, and the religion of the Third Term, being announced now.

The symbol of Judaism—a religion of the Father—is the rod hidden in the ark. Its ethic protects reproduction of the species.

The symbol of Christianity—a religion of the Son—is, on the one hand, the cross, and on the other, the sword: renunciation of the sex act and scorn for life. But in the shadow of the Christ, the worshippers of Satan make divine the womb of the woman in secret orgies, which maintain the dynamism of the march forward. The white mass of the transubstantiation is thus attenuated by the black mass of the redynamization of the flesh, which, without that, would become anemic.

The symbol of the third religion—the Religion of the Mother—is the arrow launched toward heaven. The golden mass, which it will establish, will glorify the real love of the flesh, in order to release from the latter the renovating and ascendant spirit, which will make all things new upon the earth.

Blessed are those who shall assist at this mass.

appendices

Appendix A

THE TWO EDITIONS OF THE STORY

The Sacred Rite of Magical Love was originally published in serial form in *La Flèche,* from October 15, 1930, through December 15, 1931 (the first eight issues of the newspaper). In early 1932 it was reprinted all together as a supplement to the newspaper. The two texts are identical, except for a few typographical errors, easily amended. The supplement, though, contains some things that were not in the serialization. Most notably, these are the illustration of the Aum Clock, Naglowska's preface, and the doctrinal summary at the end. This last had been published separately in *La Flèche No. 7,* before the serialization was finished.

The differences do not end there, though. The supplement contains an interesting curriculum vitae for Maria de Naglowska as a writer. Here it is, in translation.

TRANSLATIONS

Une révolution dans la philosophie, by Frank Grandjean, of
the University of Geneva (in Russian) Moscow: 1912.*

Poème à quatre voix, by Julius Evola, Rome: 1921.[†]

Raspoutine, by Simanovitch, Paris: N. R. F., 1930.

Magia Sexualis, by P. B. Randolph, Paris: Editions Robert
Telin, 1931.[‡]

IN PREPARATION

The Third Term of the Trinity

The New Ternary Rites

The Temple of Life[§]

---

*[I was able to get a pdf file of the 1916 second edition of this book from
www.archive.org. It is a 284-page work on the philosophy of Henri Bergson. It states that the first edition was translated into Russian by Mme.
Marie Naglovska, apparently the form of her name that she was using at
the time. Naglowska's attribution of her translation to 1912 is incorrect,
since the first edition came out in 1913. With regard to Bergson's evi-
dent influence on Naglowska's thinking, see appendix C. —*Trans.*]

†[This dadaistic poem was originally written by Evola in Italian, but it
has only survived in Naglowska's French translation. —*Trans.*]

‡[Naglowska did much more than just translate this work, which is
only known in her "translation." It has become the classic work on sex
magic. A new English translation is forthcoming from Inner Traditions.
—*Trans.*]

§[It is not known whether Naglowska finished these books before she
died. They were never published. —*Trans.*]

JOURNALISM

Occasional collaboration in the Swiss newspapers, 1916 to 1921.

Regular collaboration on *L'Italia,* Rome, 1921 to 1926.

Regular collaboration on *La Réforme,* Alexandria, Egypt, 1927 to 1928.

Direction and collaboration on *Alexandrie Nouvelle,* Alexandria, Egypt, 1928 to 1929.

Direction and collaboration on *La Flèche, organe d'action magique,* Paris, since 1930.

Interestingly, Naglowska neglected to mention that in 1912 she had written a French grammar for Russian immigrants to Switzerland, still available in a couple of libraries. Also, in 1918 she had reported on the Geneva peace talks, writing a report that is still available in some of the world's libraries: *La Paix et son principal obstacle* (Peace and Its Principal Obstacle).

Another difference is that the supplement version of this story had its own cover and title page. While Naglowska had used a pseudonym, Xenia Norval, in the serialization, she used her own name in the supplement. In the supplement, the title is accompanied by a subtitle, *Aveu* (Confession), and, in very large type, "26.1." The former has led many to the conclusion that the story contains autobiographical elements. The latter is simply a mystery.

My first theory with regard to "26.1" was that it referred to the Aum Clock diagram. According to the illustration, the fall is from "2" to "6," and then the ascension is from "6" to "1," giving a progression for the whole cycle of 2 - 6 - 1. Why, then, is it not written in some form such as 2.6.1, instead of 26.1. The answer, I now think, is that it doesn't refer to the Aum Clock at all.

My second theory, the one that I still favor, is that "26.1" is a biblical citation. To test this, I went through the Bible, looking for books that had a chapter 26, and reading the first verse. In only one case did I find anything appropriate, and that is Psalm 26, verse 1. It is, in fact, so fitting that it could have been carved on Naglowska's tombstone as an epitaph. I don't know which version of the Bible Naglowska kept handy, but I have chosen to quote, and translate, the French *version synodale.* It was widely available in Naglowska's time and is the most beautiful of all the French translations I've found.

> *Fais-moi justice, ô Eternel ! Car je*
> *marche dans l'intégrité.*
> *Je mets ma confiance en l'Eternel : je ne*
> *serai pas ébranlé.*

Do justice for me, Eternal One! For I
    walk in integrity.
I place my confidence in the Eternal One:
    I shall not be shaken.

Appendix B

THE AUM CLOCK

There are many things to be said about the mysterious drawing known as the "Aum Clock." First of all, the zigzag lines are very similar to the energy pathways in the *etz chaim,* or "tree of life" of the Kabbalah. The number of points connected, eleven, is even the same if one counts *Daath* (Knowledge) within the scheme of the *sephiroth.* Because I am not really a kabbalist, I'll leave this line of research to others.

It should be noted that the illustration at the beginning of the book is not quite correct: the "1 3 2" at the top, outside the circle, should be "5 3 2" to agree with the text and with Naglowska's notation in the preface that "1 = 5." Also, the first set of instructions in the text for drawing the design is evidently incorrect and produces a different, asymmetrical design that was probably not intended. Later in the story, a correct description is given.

A puzzling thing about this "clock" is that the hours

are numbered counterclockwise. I at first thought that this had been done arbitrarily and doubted that it had any real significance. Recently, though, I wanted to reproduce the design, based on the instructions in the text, and I grabbed a pad of blank astrological chart forms to make the drawing of the circle easier. Looking at the chart forms, I realized that astrological "houses," as well as signs of the zodiac, run counter-clockwise, and of course, in each case, there are twelve of them. The design illustrated and described may, therefore, be a composite one: it may reference the "tree of life" of the Kabbalah (or it may not), and at the same time it may have an astrological function.

Here, I was on firmer ground, since I have in the past been both a student and a practitioner of astrology. It was easy to come to the conclusion that the twelve "hours" must represent the twelve signs of the tropical zodiac (the one normally used by astrologers and found in astrological ephemerides). If this is true, then the most logical assumption is that the three numbers above the circle represent three transiting celestial bodies. In other words, whatever other significance the design may have, it also indicates a particular date range when three planets were passing through signs one, eleven, and twelve (Aries, Aquarius, and Pisces).

To find out what date, or date range, is indicated, we have to make an assumption about the numbering scheme used to indicate the planets. After considering several possibilities, I came up with the two schemes that seemed most likely. It should be noted that, in traditional geocentric astrology, the Earth is not counted as a planet, nor is its position shown in astrological ephemerides. Because one of the transiting planets is "3," the scheme used is not a simple numbering of the planetary orbits (unless the sun is counted as "1," in which case the earth, if counted at all, would be "4").

To make a long story shorter, I settled on two likely schemes: In the first (scheme "A"), neither the Sun nor the Earth is counted, and the numbers "1" through "5" represent in order Mercury, Venus, Mars, Jupiter, and Saturn. In the second (scheme "B"), the Sun is counted, but the Earth is not (this is more consistent with traditional, geocentric astrology), and the numbers "1" through "6" represent in order Sun, Mercury, Venus, Mars, Jupiter, and Saturn.

Scheme "A" gives the following date ranges (when Venus, Mars, and Saturn are in the proper signs):

Jan. 24 to Jan 29, 1938,

Dec. 26, 1939 to Jan. 3, 1940.

Scheme "B"gives the following date range (when Mercury, Venus, and Jupiter are in the proper zodiacal signs):

Jan. 26. 1940 to Feb. 11, 1940.

In addition, the Scheme "A" conditions could have been fulfilled in 1967, 1996, and may be fulfilled in 2025.

The Scheme "B" conditions had the possibility of being fulfilled in 1951, 1963, 1975, 1987, and 1999. All three conditions were not fulfilled in the period Jan. 22, 2011, to June 4, 2011, though there was a very impressive stellium in Aries during that period. There is a possibility that all three conditions may be fulfilled sometime in 2022. I leave the refinement of this research to others.

The 1938 to 1940 dates are suggestive of the start of World War II, but they do not agree with specific major events, such as the invasion of Poland or the fall of Paris. They also do not agree with Naglowska's own prediction. She expected the war to start in 1936 (which was actually the start of the Spanish Civil War, the preamble to WWII).

Undoubtedly, many will wonder whether Naglowska could have gotten this astrological information or done these calculations. The answer is that she did not have to do it herself. One of the best-known French astrologers, Jean Carteret, was a member of Naglowska's group, *La Confrérie de la Flèche d'Or.*[*1]

---

*[We are informed of this fact by Marc Pluquet, in *La Sophiale*. —*Trans.*]

Appendix C
NAGLOWSKA'S
SOURCES

Maria de Naglowska claimed to have received one of the essential parts of her teaching, that of the successive eras of the Father, of the Son, and of the Holy Spirit from an old monk when she was in Rome. Specifically, she said that she received this teaching when Pope Pius XI was being elected as the new pope. Because the papal election took place on February 6, 1922, we have an exact date. What we do not know is who the old monk was.

The teaching of the three successive eras associated with the three persons of the Trinity can be traced back to an old monk who lived in the twelfth and early thirteenth centuries, Joachim of Fiore. He taught that the time from Adam to Christ was associated with the Father and the Old Testament; from Christ to a time yet to come (probably in the thirteenth century) he gave to the Son and the New Testament; these would be followed by an era of the Holy Spirit, which would in turn be followed by the end of the world.*

Obviously, we have several possibilities here. Naglowska may have encountered the teachings of Joachim of Fiore through a book, or she may have met a follower in person or through one of his followers. In the latter case, the name of Eugene Vintras comes to mind.† Vintras had a form of this teaching of the three eras. But because Vintras died eight years before Naglowska was born, any influence from Vintras would have had to be indirect. It could have come from Eliphas Levi, who wrote about Vintras in his *History of Magic*. This is rather likely, because there is other evidence of the influence of Levi on Naglowska.‡ Or the influence may have come from Vintras himself through his 700-page work, *L'Evangile Eternel*. Nor does this exhaust the possibilities,

---

*[Joachim of Fiore had a nice illustration of this system in his *Book of Figures*, and it is conveniently reproduced for us in the book *Apocalyptic Spirituality*, translation and introduction by Bernard McGinn, preface by Marjorie Reeves. —*Trans.*]

†[The best and fairest source I have found for information on Vintras is the book *Vintras Hérésiarque et Prophète*, by Maurice Garçon. —*Trans.*]

‡[For example, the division of his work, *The Book of Splendors*, into three parts, dealing with the Zohar, Christianity, and "The Flaming Star" (Freemasonry). In Naglowska's system the flaming star is also a symbol for the third era. Naglowska need not, however, have gotten this symbol from Levi, because there is some evidence that she may have been a Co-Mason. —*Trans.*]

because there were followers of Vintras in Paris while Naglowska was living there.*

But we do not have to assume that Naglowska knew of Joachim of Fiore, Vintras, and *l'Evangile Eternel* because she mentioned all of them herself. The lead article in issue number eleven of *La Flèche,* for March 15, 1932, is Naglowska's review of an anti-Masonic book by J. Marques-Riviere.[†1] The review can be called a solid defense of Freemasonry, but it was occasioned by Marques-Riviere's attack on Naglowska's magical group. Two pages of his book are taken up by an extract from *La Flèche.* In fact, Naglowska tells us right where to look: it starts on page 175.

Naglowska may have gotten a seed-idea from Joachim of Fiore and Eugene Vintras, but she gave it her own spin. With them it was apocalyptic, a one-time thing; with her it was a cosmic concept, cyclic, repeated incessantly. That is one example of the ways in which her vision is more universal, and more timeless than theirs.

Another concept that is typical of Naglowska's writing is her distrust of human reason and its limitations, in favor of

---

*[For example, J. Bricaud, who owned an occult bookstore in Paris and was involved with many occult groups. It is inconceivable that Naglowska, who spent most of her afternoons with occultists, would not have known Bricaud. —*Trans.*]

†[*La Trahison Spirituelle de la F∴ M∴* —*Trans.*]

what she called "direct intelligence" or "direct understanding." She inadvertently revealed to us the source of this idea in the front matter of the 1932 supplemental edition of *The Sacred Rite of Magical Love.** It was a book that she translated into Russian before the first World War: *Une révolution dans la philosophie,* by Frank Grandjean.† This is a book about the philosophy of Henri Bergson, and it is clear that it had a significant influence on Naglowska's thinking.

Bergson's main thesis was that reason alone, due to its limitations, was not to be trusted, and that intuition was necessary for the understanding of life. This idea is echoed many times in Naglowska's books.

Naglowska also adopted one of Bergson's philosophical terms, *Duration.* In Bergson's system, Duration = free will = pure mobility; in Naglowska's, it is the struggle between the Light and Dark forces, the "Will to Live" and the "Will to Die."

An even deeper connection between Bergson and Naglowska lies in their respect for mysticism. Bergson expressed it this way:

On earth, in any case, the species that is the reason for existence of all the others is only partially itself. It would

---

*[See appendix A. —*Trans.*]

†[See introduction, endnote 1. —*Trans.*]

never even have occurred to it to become completely itself if certain of its representatives had not succeeded, through an individual effort that is over and above the general work of living, in breaking the resistance of the instrument, in triumphing over materiality, and finally in finding God. These people are the mystics. They have opened a way for others to follow. They have, in so doing, shown the philosopher where life comes from and where it is going.[2]

Bergson goes on to say, in his next chapter:

The dynamic religion that thus arises is opposed to static religion, born of the story-telling function, as open society is opposed to closed society.[3]

It is possible that Bergson's philosophy and Naglowska's new religion both had their origin in a mystical experience. In Naglowska's case, she has done her best to tell us about it in this book and in the others that she wrote. It falls to us to listen, translating as best we can the necessarily symbolic language of the mystic.

NOTES

INTRODUCTION.
A LIFE OF MAGIC AND MYSTERY

1. Frank Grandjean, *Une révolution dans la philosophie* (Geneva: Librairie Atar and Paris: Librairie Félix Alcan, 1916), xii.

2. Aron Simanovitch, *Raspoutine*, translated by S. de Leo and Mme de Naglowska (Paris: Librairie Gallimard for NRF), 1930.

3. Pascal Beverly Randolph, *Magia Sexualis*, compiled and translated by Maria de Naglowska (Paris: Robert Télin), 1931.

4. Maria de Naglowska, *La Lumière du sexe* (Paris: Éditions de la Flèche, 1932).

5. Maria de Naglowska, *The Light of Sex*, translated by Donald Traxler (Rochester, Vt.: Inner Traditions, 2011).

6. Maria de Naglowska, *Le mystère de la pendaison* (Paris: Éditions de la Flèche, 1934).

7. Maria de Naglowska, *Advanced Sex Magic* (Rochester, Vt.: Inner Traditions, 2011).

APPENDIX B.
THE AUM CLOCK

1. Marc Pluquet, *La Sophiale: Maria de Naglowska, sa vie – son oeuvre* (Montpeyroux: Éditions Gouttelettes de Rosée, n.d.,) 7.

APPENDIX C.
NAGLOWSKA'S SOURCES

1. Jean Marquès-Rivière, *La trahison spirituelle de la F∴M∴* (Paris: Éditions des Portiques, 1931), 175–77.
2. Henri Bergson, *Les deux sources de la morale et de la religion* (Paris: Librairie Félix Alcan, 1932), 276. [Translation of excerpt by Donald Traxler.]
3. Ibid., 289.

BIBLIOGRAPHY

Alexandrian, Sarane. *Les libérateurs de l'amour.* Paris: Éditions du Seuil, 1977.

Anel-Kham, B. (pseudonym of Henri Meslin). *Théorie et pratique de la magie sexuelle.* Paris: Librairie Astra, 1938.

Barnstone, Willis, editor. *The Other Bible.* San Francisco: Harper & Row, 1984.

Bergson, Henri. *Les deux sources de la morale et de la religion.* Paris: Librairie Félix Alcan, 1932.

Deveney, John Patrick, and Franklin Rosemont. *Paschal Beverly Randolph: A Nineteenth-Century Black American Spiritualist.* Albany: SUNY Press, 1997.

Evola, Julius. *The Metaphysics of Sex.* New York: Inner Traditions International, 1983. Reprint, *Eros and the Mysteries of Love,* Rochester, Vt.: 1991.

Evola, Julius, and the Ur Group. *Introduction to Magic.* Rochester, Vt.: Inner Traditions, 2001.

Garçon, Maurice. *Vintras, hérésiarque et prophète.* Paris: Librairie Critique Émile Nourry, 1928.

Gengenbach, Ernest de. *L'Expérience démoniaque.* Paris: Eric Losfeld, 1968.

Geyraud, Pierre (pseudonym of l'Abbé Pierre Guyader). *Les petites églises de Paris*. Paris: Éditions Émile-Paul Frères, 1937.

Grandjean, Frank. *Une révolution dans la philosophie*. Geneva: Librairie Atar; Paris: Librairie Félix Alcan, 1916.

Hakl, Hans Thomas. "Maria de Naglowska and the Confrérie de la Flèche d'Or." *Politica Hermetica* 20 (2006): 113–23.

Marquès-Rivière, Jean. *La trahison de la spirituelle F.·. M.·.* Paris: Éditions des Portiques, 1931.

Naglowska, Maria de. *Advanced Sex Magic: The Hanging Mystery Initiation*. Translated by Donald Traxler. Rochester, Vt.: Inner Traditions, 2011.

———. *La Flèche Organe d'Action Magique* 1–20 (15 Oct. 1930–15 Jan. 1935).

———. *La Lumière du sexe*. Paris: Éditions de la Flèche, 1932.

———. *Le Mystère de la pendaison*. Paris: Éditions de la Flèche, 1934.

———. *Le Rite sacré de l'amour magique: Aveu 26.1*. Paris: Supplément de *La Flèche: Organe d'Action Magique*, 1932.

———. *The Light of Sex*. Translated by Donald Traxler. Rochester, Vt.: Inner Traditions, 2011.

Pluquet, Marc. *La Sophiale: Maria de Naglowska, sa vie – son oeuvre*. Montpeyroux: Éditions Gouttelettes de Rosée, n.d.

Randolph, Paschal Beverly. *Magia Sexualis*. Compiled and translated by Maria de Naglowska. Paris: Robert Télin, 1931.

Schreck, Nikolas, and Zeena. *Demons of the Flesh*. Clerkenwell: Creation Books, 2002.

Simanovitch, Aron. *Raspoutine*. Translated by S. de Leo and Mme de Naglowska. Paris: Librairie Gallimard for NRF, 1930.

Thimmy, René (pseudonym of M. Magre). *La Magie à Paris.* Paris: Les Éditions de France, 1934.

Vintras, Eugène. *L'Évangile éternel.* London: Trubner & Co., 1857; reprinted, Charleston, S.C.: Nabu Press, 2010.

INDEX

1, 5–6, 32

2, 3, 5–6

3, 5–6

4, 3, 4

5, 3–4

6, 3, 4, 69

7, 4–5

8, 3, 4

9, 69, 70–71

10, 3–4

11, 3, 5–6

12, 5–6, 32

26.1, 102

36, 68

41, 68–69

77, 68–69

Adam, 16

*Advanced Sex Magic: The
    Hanging Mystery Initiation,*
    xiv–xv

Apouchtine, 63–64

apple, 16

ark, 95

arrow, 96

astrological houses, 105–7

AUM clock, 32, 102, 104

    event dating and, 104–7

    as key, 1–6

    Xenia's creation of, 42–48

ballroom, 21, 57–62

Baptism, the, 28–38

Bergson, Henri, 111–12

Birth to Love, 15–27

cardinal directions, 25–27

Carteret, Jean, 105

Catholics and Catholicism,
    21–23

Caucasus, 9–12

children, 8

Christianity, 95–96

clocks. *See* AUM clock

clothing, 28–29, 40–41, 54–55

colored lights, 83–84

Cossacks, 77

courage, 53, 80

cross, 70–71, 95

Crossing, 72–81

crown of wildflowers, 30, 41

dancing, 59–61

Death, 16, 26

direct intelligence, 109

Divine Triangle, 5–6

division, 93

Doctrine of the Third Term of
    the Trinity, xiv, 93–96

Don Cossacks, 77

dreams, 30–32

Duration, 111

Earth, 104

east, 25–27, 50–51

eight, 3, 4

eleven, 3, 5–6

Entry, 3

Eve, 16

Evil, 31

Evola, Julius, xi

Fall, 2, 93

Father, 2, 93–96

five, 3–4

food, 24

forty-one, 68–69

four, 3, 4

free will, 111

Garden of Eden, 16

gold, 84

golden mass, 96

Grandjean, Frank, 111

Grob, Marie, xv

Group of Ur, xi

happiness, 7

Hé, 89

Heaven, 22

Hé-Hô-Là, 89–90

History of Magic, 109

Hô, 89

holy icons, 21–23

Holy Spirit, xii, 108–9

Hopenko, Moise, x

houses, orientation of, 25–27

human body, 26–27

immobility, 25

Infinite, 24

influence, 22–24
intellect, 25
In the Mist of Thought,
    7–14

Joachim of Fiore, 108–9, 110
Joy on the Plain, 49–71
Judaism, 21–23, 95
Jupiter, 106

Kabbalah, 104
Khlysti, sect of, xii
kissing, 14, 16, 74–75
Kremmerz, Giuliano, xi

La, 89
La Flèche, 99, 110
L'Evangile Eternel, 109–10
Levi, Eliphas, 109
liberation, 56–57, 68
Life, 26, 57
Light of Sex, The, xiv–xv
lights, colored, 83–84
love, birth of, 17–27

Magia Sexualis, xiii–xiv
Magician, 23
Marques-Riviere, J., 110
Mars, 106

Master, the, 9–14, 87–91
Mercury, 106
Metaphysics of Sex, The, xiii
mirrors, 29–30, 41–42
Misha
    crossing and, 72–81
    joy on the plain and, 51,
        58–71
    on the other shore, 82–92
    Xenia's virginity and, 33–38,
        44
modesty, 56
molitva, 22–24
Morning Star, 6
Mother, 2, 93–96
multiplicity, 93
mysticism, 111–12

Naglowska, Maria de
    background of, ix–xvi
    sources of, 108–12
    works of, 99–103
nature, 15–20
Niania, 51
nine, 69, 70–71
normalcy, 7–8
north, 25–27
Norval, Xenia, ix, 101
nostalgia, 93

obedience, 50–51, 53

one, 5–6, 32

On the Other Shore, 82–92

Origin, 93

Orthodox, 21–23

passivity, 51, 53

Past, 8–9

perfumes, 84

Pius XI, Pope, 108

powerlessness, 19

prayer, 22–24

prison, 70–71

Psalms, Book of, 102–103

purity, 56–57

Randolph, Paschal Beverly,
    xiii–xiv

Rasputin, xii

reality, 15

reason, 110–11

Rebirth, 26, 89

red river of animal life, 80–81

Renewal, 2

rod, 95

Root of Eternal Things, 53

saber, 67, 76–77, 80–81

Sacred Triangle, 89

sacrifice, 74

Satan

    Naglowska and, xii–xiii

    Son and, 93

    true name of, 8–14

Saturn, 106

Scheme A, 106–7

Scheme B, 106–7

science, 15

Seal of Solomon, 3

Second Marriage, 6

sect of the Khlysti, xii

Serge-of-the-Many-Miracles,
    St., 23

seven, 4–5

seventy-seven, 68–69

sex and sexuality, 56–57

Shadow, 16

shame, 56–57, 70

six, 3, 4, 69

sleep, 30–32

Society, 57

Son, 2, 93–96

south, 25–27

strength, 19

Sun, 12, 106

ten, 3–4

Terek, 80

Test, the, 39–48
Third Term of the Trinity, xiv,
    93–96
thirty-six, 68
three, 5–6
translations, 100
Traxler, Donald, ix–xvii
tree of life, 105
Trinity, xii, 5–6
trinity, 93–96
Truth, 57, 91–92
twelve, 5–6, 32
two, 3, 5–6

Unique Spirit, 93
Unjust, 70
Unknown, 73
Ur, Group of, xi

Venus, 104
Victorious Ones, 4–5
Vintras, Eugene, 109–10
virginity, 44

Wassilkowsky, Misha
    crossing and, 72–81

joy on the plain and, 51,
    58–71
on the other shore, 82–92
Xenia's virginity and, 33–38,
    44
Wassilkowsky family, 28
west, 25–27
Wicked One, 87
will, 81
Will to Die, 111
Will to Live, 111
wind, 62
World War II, 107

Xenophonta
    AUM clock and, 42–48
    baptism of, 28–38
    crossing and, 72–81
    joy on plain and, 49–71
    Master and, 9–14
    Misha and, 34–38, 57–71
    on the other shore, 82–92
    test of, 39–48
    virginity loss of, 33–38, 39–41

zodiac, 105–7

BOOKS OF RELATED INTEREST

The Light of Sex
Initiation, Magic, and Sacrament
by Maria de Naglowska

Advanced Sex Magic
The Hanging Mystery Initiation
by Maria de Naglowska

The Lost Art of Enochian Magic
Angels, Invocations, and the Secrets Revealed to Dr. John Dee
by John DeSalvo, Ph.D.

Introduction to Magic
Rituals and Practical Techniques for the Magus
by Julius Evola and the UR Group

Eros and the Mysteries of Love
The Metaphysics of Sex
by Julius Evola

The Complete Illustrated Kama Sutra
Edited by Lance Dane

The Secret History of Western Sexual Mysticism
Sacred Practices and Spiritual Marriage
by Arthur Versluis

William Blake's Sexual Path to Spiritual Vision
by Marsha Keith Schuchard

INNER TRADITIONS • BEAR & COMPANY
P.O. Box 388
Rochester, VT 05767
1-800-246-8648
www.InnerTraditions.com

Or contact your local bookseller